M000237546

IMAGES
of America
FAIRFAX

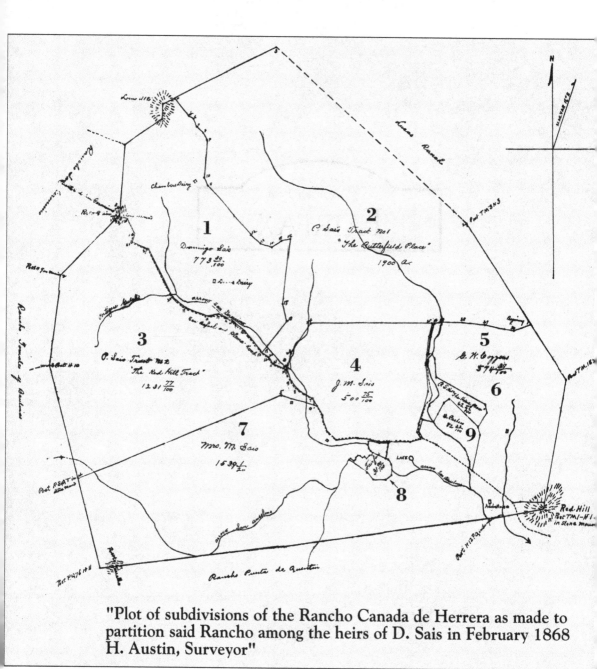

"Plot of subdivisions of the Rancho Canada de Herrera as made to partition said Rancho among the heirs of D. Sais in February 1868 H. Austin, Surveyor"

The names and acreages designated on the map are as follows: 1) Dominga Sais, 773.30 acres; 2) P. Sais Tract No. 1, The Butterfield Place, 1,900 acres; 3) P. Sais Tract No. 2, The Red Hill Tract, 1,231.77 acres; 4) J. M. Sais, 500.75 acres; 5) G. W. Cozzens, 574.37 acres; 6) A. Sais, The Home Place, 62.22 acres; 7) Mrs. M. Sais 1,539.05 acres; 8)Fairfax, 31.90 acres; 9) S. Pacheco, 82.31 acres. The total of these figures equals 6,695.67 acres, slightly more than the original land grant of 6,658.35—a surplus of 37.32 acres.

IMAGES
of America

FAIRFAX

William and Brian Sagar

ARCADIA
PUBLISHING

Copyright © 2005 by William Sagar and Brian Sagar
ISBN 978-1-5316-1698-4

Published by Arcadia Publishing
Charleston, South Carolina

Library of Congress Catalog Card Number: 2005934919

For all general information contact Arcadia Publishing at:
Telephone 843-853-2070
Fax 843-853-0044
E-mail sales@arcadiapublishing.com
For customer service and orders:
Toll-Free 1-888-313-2665

Visit us on the Internet at www.arcadiapublishing.com

An aerial view of downtown Fairfax in 1938 shows, at top, the race track built in 1930, where 1932 Olympic hopefuls practiced, complete with a grandstand for spectators. The upper part of the track is now the Little League ball field. The lower left is where the 1st Cavalry camped out in 1883. (Courtesy of the Fairfax Historical Society collection.)

CONTENTS

ACKNOWLEDGMENTS

On behalf of the Fairfax Historical Society, the authors wish to thank all the past and present members who have generously loaned photographs to the society over the past 17 years for copying and/or safekeeping and additions to our archives, which have made this book possible. We must acknowledge the herculean efforts of the late William "Bill" Allen, who dedicated his life to the pursuit of Fairfax history, pouring through books and newspapers and documenting all the information he could find through the many publications to which he contributed over his lifetime. Much of the information contained herein is the result of his efforts.

We also wish to thank the following individuals and societies who have contributed to our knowledge of Fairfax and its vicinity: Charmaine Burdell; Charles Gay of Batesville, Virginia; Chuck Grasso; Robert Madison of Alexandria, Virginia; Marin County Free Library, Anne T. Kent California Room; Marin County Historical Society; Jocelyn Moss; Richard Snowden Samuels of Evanston, Illinois; Sausalito Historical Society; Newall Snyder; Gunard Solberg; Sharon Springett; Nancy Thiessen of Laurel, Maryland; Laurie Thompson; and the Virginia Historical Society of Richmond, Virginia.

In addition, the authors would like to thank Brad Breithaupt and Sharon Sagar for their editorial review and support of this project.

Our sincere thanks to the many donors among our members and friends, not listed above, who have helped with photographs and bits of information over the years, some of whom are credited among the captions.

INTRODUCTION

Nestled in the heart of Marin County at the upper end of Ross Valley, the Town of Fairfax still retains its small-town charm and atmosphere. Its location provides easy access to San Francisco and the commercial corridor of Marin, while providing a close-knit feel for its residents. The valleys and hills that comprise the town provide a strong sense of community and uniqueness, which attract a strong artistic and entrepreneurial citizenry, who resist the influence of outside mega-conglomerates.

Travel back to the earliest days of Fairfax. Meet the town namesake, who rejected his rightful title as an English lord to become a local politician. Meet the residents who appreciated the beauty of the surrounding area on their visits and decided to move to Fairfax year-round, many establishing small community businesses. Discover the diverse people who came to build a town around a scenic rail line. Enjoy special moments as the town discovered many unique opportunities that have created a lively and well-loved place that makes everyone feel like they are home.

The earliest inhabitants of Marin County were the Coastal Miwok Indians, who freely roamed the hills and valleys of the beautiful unspoiled countryside. They often hunted in the interior valleys along the creeks and streams. The area, now known as Fairfax, was an ideal area for them to visit and there is evidence that they frequented areas, such as the grounds around where the Fairfax Pavilion currently sits. Artifacts, such as a grinding stone and arrowheads, have been found there, as well as along creeks and trails that were probably frequented on their journeys.

The Miwok's lives were changed when the Russians and Spanish missionaries settled in their midst. The influence of religion and the changes to their lifestyle, as well as the influx of Caucasian settlers, ultimately led to the decline of Marin's earliest residents.

Mission San Rafael Arcangel was the 20th mission established in California by the Franciscans. The mission, founded in 1817, taught the American Indians many skills, including ranching and herding cattle. It was also during this time that enormous areas of land were granted to those who had served the Mexican government well. One of these grantees was Domingo Sais who was given the tract known as Canada de Herrera in 1839.

This land tract of 6,658 acres covered the area now known as Fairfax and about one-half of San Anselmo. The area was soon split into smaller land plots and was either sold or given to many prominent Marin residents, including some of the earliest Fairfax settlers, such as Dr. Alfred Taliferro and his friend, Lord Charles Fairfax, the town's namesake.

Take a photographic journey from the earliest days of these Fairfax settlers; enjoy the downtown streets as they evolved from the earliest shops to a vital stop along the railroad route. Meet some of the residents who helped to establish Fairfax as a vital community, from the Italian workers who came to build the Alpine Dam on the outskirts of Fairfax, refugees from the San Francisco earthquake in 1906, as well as the many Bay Area residents who came to Fairfax to vacation at the idyllic Marin Town and Country Club.

Explore the establishment of the town schools, churches, and a women's tuberculosis sanatorium, and catch a glimpse of an Olympic-sized track field. Travel up the Incline Railroad to explore the hillside then explore the movie-making industry that captured Fairfax's earliest days.

The authors, a father-and-son team, have culled several private photograph collections, as well as many from the local historical society, to give you a comprehensive photographic diary of Fairfax, from it's earliest days through the mid-1940s. Enjoy discovering the many Fairfax moments that have led to the creation of this unique Marin town.

Over the years, many artifacts associated with the Coastal Miwok tribe, the earliest inhabitants of the Fairfax area, have been found. In this photomontage are clamshells, left, discovered on the banks of the creek below the pavilion. The three obsidian arrowheads were found in various areas of town. The small mortar at the lower right may have been used to make face decorations for ceremonial occasions. It was discovered in a Fairfax creek. The large mortar and pestle were discovered near the pavilion. These are among the many reminders of the Coastal Miwoks who lived and traveled in the Fairfax area, and much of the County of Marin, for many years before the more recent residents mentioned in this book.

One

DOMINGO SAIS

Among the first residents of the area known today as the Town of Fairfax was a Mexican citizen by the name of Domingo Sais, his wife, Manuella, and their five children, Jose, Pedro, Dolores, Vincenta, and Jose. The children were baptized at Mission Dolores in San Francisco.

Domingo Sais was born in California and baptized at Mission La Purisima in Lompoc in 1806. He was a Mexican soldier in the San Francisco Presidio from 1826 to 1833 and, in 1837, at the age of 31, was a soldier in the San Francisco militia.

It was common for the Mexican government to reward their soldiers with a gift of land in lieu of pay and, in 1839, Domingo was released from duty and granted 6,658.35 acres in what is now all of the Town of Fairfax and almost half of the neighboring town of San Anselmo.

Available records indicate that the first five offspring were born in San Francisco and came to this area with Domingo and his wife. Six more children were born in Marin County—Ygnacia, Jesus, Dominga (who died young), Jose, Lucy, and Dominga. The names of Pedro, their second son, and Dominga, the youngest daughter, are usually mentioned in real estate transactions after Domingo's death.

Through marriages of his offspring, the Sais name became connected with such well-known Marin families as the Blacks, Bournes, Burdells, Castros, Pachecos, and Peraltas. In time, Dominga, the youngest of Domingo's offspring, came of age and assumed some of the duties of managing the Sais land interests with the help of her brother-in-law, Salvadore Pacheco. Manuella arranged the lease of land to the North Pacific Coast Railroad in 1875 for the picnic grounds, which became known as Fairfax Park.

Sais family activities were largely agricultural in nature. They raised produce, horses, cows, beef cattle, sheep and, no doubt, some chickens—all products to sustain themselves, with possibly some surplus to sell. The entire valley was sparsely populated and cattle outnumbered people by a very large margin. Until the early 1900s, there were only five or six homes in the upper valley, known today as Ross Valley.

After Domingo Sais's death in 1853, the land was divided among his heirs. As new settlers came into the county, ownership was changed again and again until its believed that little, if any, of the original land grant remains in the hands of a Sais descendant. The thousands of citizens who have moved into this favored land called Fairfax now own the property.

Canada de Herrera, shown above, was one of the 25 Mexican land grants into which Marin County was divided. The Canada de Herrera land was granted to Domingo Sais on August 10, 1839, giving him claim to 6,658.35 acres. (Courtesy of the Fairfax Historical Society collection.)

The only known photograph of a member of the immediate family of Domingo Sais is this one of his daughter Dominga, with her husband, Joseph Bresson, possibly in a wedding portrait. At the age of 18, Dominga married Joseph in 1871. They had three children: John, Mary, and Louise. Dominga and Joseph owned and ran the 700-acre ranch in the western part of the original land grant. (Courtesy of the W. Wilson collection.)

Although this photograph is inscribed "At Lepori's Fairfax, April 13, 1907," it should also be noted as an early home of Joseph and Dominga Sais Bresson, who lived here from 1884 until the early 1890s. Since they are the earliest known residents, it is possible they built the home. It is one of the oldest and most historically significant dwellings in Fairfax and still stands at 10 Olema Road. In 1894, Dominga sold the 10-acre plot on which this home was built to George Dickson. The Leporis bought the plot from the Dickson estate in 1899, then in 1906 leased eight acres to Carlet and Tiereslin for construction of the White House Resort across the creek from Manor Station. The eight acres were sold to the Fairfax Development Company in 1912 for the subdivision known as Fairfax Manor. In 1911, the Lepori house, on the remaining two acres, was leased to P. Recomi, who established and ran a restaurant in the basement. By 1937, the Leporis had left and another restaurant, Duke's Manor Villa, was open for business in the house. In 1938, the property was sold to Mario and Rosa de Martini, who built a warehouse next to the house for their Alpine Beer Distribution Company. In the early 1950s, Rosa turned the warehouse into a restaurant, Alpine Villa, which later became Rubini's and finally Mandarin Gardens, both restaurants. (Courtesy of the Fairfax Historical Society collection.)

Two

ALFRED TALIAFERRO

Alfred Taliaferro, one of thousands who came west in the gold rush of 1849, arrived through the Golden Gate on the sailing ship *Glenmore* on October 6, 1849, after a six-month journey around the tip of South America from Richmond, Virginia. He was only 22 at the time. Contrary to the general migration of new arrivals though, he did not head for the gold fields, but rather came to the San Rafael area with several friends and rented land from Timothy Murphy for farming.

Farming was not his full time occupation, for he had been educated as a physician and practiced part of the time. There were just over 300 inhabitants in the county in 1850, hardly enough on which to build a medical practice. As the population grew, however, so did his clientele and he soon became well-known and revered in Marin County. His office and home were on Fourth Street in San Rafael, where he also later established the first drugstore in the county. He would often be seen racing along country trails, day or night, to administer to an ailing patient. Many babies delivered by him were named Alfred in his honor. He had no regard for money and would often charge a fee only if he felt the patient could afford his services, which were always given without hesitation.

In 1853, he was appointed the official doctor for San Quentin Prison. He also took part in local politics, becoming a Marin state assemblyman from 1851 to 1852. He was also a member of the first county jury and first grand jury.

He enjoyed frequent outings on horseback and often traveled to Domingo Sais's lands in the upper end of the valley. A secluded glen attracted his attention as a possible retreat from the active San Rafael area and he mentioned his feelings about the spot to Domingo. Domingo, in turn, said he would be honored to have the good doctor as a neighbor and gave him a 32-acre parcel. Taliaferro built a home, said to be a duplicate of his Virginia home, on what is now known as the former site of the Marin Town and Country Club, a virtual wilderness at that time. A few years later in 1855, his boyhood friend, Charles Fairfax and wife, Ada, visited the doctor at his country estate. They expressed such great admiration for the property that he gave it to the newly married couple as a wedding gift.

In 1878, with several other influential San Rafael citizens, Taliaferro organized the purchase of 112 acres west of San Rafael to establish the Mt. Tamalpais Cemetery. His death in December 1885 stunned Bay Area residents. The business district of San Rafael closed down for his funeral, as virtually the entire community turned out, followed by a procession to his burial site at the cemetery. Prominent city and county officials, including judges and supervisors, were in attendance. A well-respected individual had been lost to the community.

This portrait of Alfred W. Taliaferro was taken during his days in San Rafael. (Courtesy of the Anne T. Kent California Room, Marin County Free Library collection.)

This memorial stone bust of Alfred Taliaferro is located in a niche on a rock outcropping near his gravesite in the San Rafael cemetery he established. (Courtesy of the Brian Sagar collection.)

Alfred W. Taliaferro M.D.
A Native of Virginia
Died at San Rafael
Dec. 9, 1885
He rests from his labors,
and his works do follow him.

14

Three

CHARLES SNOWDEN FAIRFAX

In 1560, Thomas Fairfax of Denton became the 1st Lord Fairfax in British nobility. The title was carried down through succeeding generations to the 5th Lord Thomas, 1657–1710. He was the first of the family to come to the New World and the Virginia Colony where his wife, Catherine Culpepper, had become heiress to property rights covering more than five million acres in Virginia in 1660.

Some writings have stated that this acreage would become Virginia, when in reality it was just the upper part of the eventual state. It was still a sizable piece of real estate, which a young George Washington, at age 16, would survey for the 6th Lord Thomas Fairfax.

Four generations later, in 1829, Charles Snowden Fairfax was born at Vaucluse, the estate of the 9th Lord Thomas, in what is now Alexandria, Virginia. Charles's parents were Albert Fairfax and Caroline Snowden. Since Albert died before the death of his father, the 9th Lord Thomas, the title was passed on to Charles Snowden Fairfax, or the entitlement thereto.

To have accepted the title as the 10th Lord, Baron of Cameron, Charles would have been required to denounce his U.S. citizenship and return to England. He refused to do so and on his death in 1869, the title passed to his brother, John Contee Fairfax, as the 11th Lord Fairfax. John did not accept the title either, which then moved on to his son, Albert Kirby Fairfax. Albert accepted the honor and became 12th Lord Fairfax when he returned to England in the early 1900s. Two more generations have brought the title to today's 14th Lord Nicholas Fairfax of London.

On April 6, 1849, Charles Snowden Fairfax, still the potential 10th Lord Fairfax, joined the company of 74 other gold seekers and left Richmond, Virginia, for a six-month journey to San Francisco on the sailing ship *Glenmore*. The first news of Charlie (as friends called him) in California was a report of his visit to Grass Valley in December 1849, traveling with his cousin "Uncle Dick" Snowden and others to a winter camp.

Charles Fairfax had been accustomed to a rather leisurely life in Virginia. The family slaves performed the physical labor—a way of life, especially for nobility. Thrust into the life of a miner in the mother lode of California during winter, must have been somewhat of a shock to Charlie, but he probably relished the thrill of the adventure and stuck with it for a while. There are stories of him working for others, pushing a wheelbarrow, or tending a mule pulling a cart of gravel and wallowing in the mud of the diggings. He must have thought there was a better way to find a fortune.

In 1851, he discovered his new calling—politics—and became a delegate to the Democratic State Convention. By 1853, he was an assemblyman from Yuba and Sierra counties and, in 1854, became Speaker of the House in Sacramento.

In 1854, he spent some time in San Francisco, as did a charming young lady by the name of Ada Benham. On January 10, 1855, they were married at the home of Ada's stepsister Henrietta Prentice in Louisville, Kentucky.

After their marriage and return to San Francisco, Charles and Ada visited Dr. Alfred Taliaferro in his country home. They expressed their great admiration of Taliaferro's estate, and Charles's boyhood friend gave them the property as a wedding gift. Thus, in 1855, the couple became residents in what would later become the Town of Fairfax.

Charles and Ada made many improvements to their new property. Charlie imported game birds to satisfy his zeal for hunting and improve his chances for success. Ada planted trees and flowers around the home and grounds and named the estate Bird's Nest Glen. It is not clear how much of their home was previously built by Taliaferro, or how much the newlyweds added, but it soon became a social center among their many friends due to their generous southern hospitality, which was enjoyed by persons from all walks of life. They entertained lavishly and it became so customary for their friends to say, "Let's go over to the Fairfaxes" or "Let's go to Fairfax" that the area took on the identity of Fairfax, which continued long after their departure, up to the time of incorporation of the town in 1931.

Charlie's potential to become Lord Fairfax followed him for years as friends admiringly addressed him as lord, which he accepted somewhat jokingly, not taking it seriously and often stating that it would never happen. Ada, however, enjoyed being referred to as Lady Fairfax. She was truly a lady of royal bearing and demeanor and both of them had a following of admiring friends, except of course, for some of Charlie's political antagonists.

Charles became Marin County supervisor in 1865 and, in 1868, was nominated as a delegate to the Democratic National Convention, held on the Fourth of July in New York City. The usual way of travel to the East Coast was via the Panama Canal, a four-week journey, so he probably left in early June. After the convention, he stayed on and visited friends and relatives in Virginia and Maryland. On April 4, 1869, he died in Baltimore, Maryland, while visiting his mother. He is buried in Rock Creek Cemetery in Washington, D.C.

Ada sold Bird's Nest Glen in 1870 and moved to Fort Ross. Charles and James Dixon had bought the fort property for its lumber potential in 1867. Ada lived there for three years, entertaining guests with her traditional Southern hospitality as long as funds would allow. In 1873, she sold the property and moved back to San Francisco. Ada's mother and a niece lived with her at Fort Ross and were noted in San Francisco directories as residents of San Francisco until her mother's death on June 22, 1884. The lack of Ada's name in later directories seems to indicate she had already moved to Washington, D.C., where she had accepted a position as official hostess in the White House. Ada died on September 26, 1888, in Washington, D.C., and is buried with Charles.

Citizens of the Town of Fairfax can be proud of its almost royal heritage, as residents of one of very few towns in California with such a noble background.

The Fairfax coat of arms, a plaque presented to the Fairfax Historical Society by the Honorable Hugh Fairfax, great-great nephew of Charles Snowden Fairfax, brother of the 14th Lord Nicholas Fairfax of London. (Courtesy of the Fairfax Historical Society collection.)

This is the only known portrait of Charles Snowden Fairfax, perhaps the basis for the sketch on the following page. Had he given up his U.S. citizenship and returned to England, Charles could have accepted the title as 10th Lord Fairfax, Baron of Cameron. He remained loyal to the country of his birth and remained here, never accepting the honor. (Courtesy of Fairfax Historical Society collection.)

These sketches of Ada and Charles Fairfax, published as part of a newspaper article in the *San Francisco Examiner* on January 1, 1893, were entitled "Our Only Baronial Estate—The Only Resident English Lord That California Ever Had." The drawings were made from photographs and the inscription, "From Ada Fairfax," was said to have been written by Lady Fairfax. (Courtesy of the Fairfax Historical Society collection.)

This gold watch was given to Charles Fairfax in May 1868 shortly before he left to attend the Fourth of July National Democratic Convention held in New York City. The inscription reads, "Hon. Chas. S. Fairfax from his California friends, May 1868." The watch is now in London, a keepsake of the Fairfax family. (Courtesy of the Hugh Fairfax collection.)

Ada Benham Fairfax is pictured around 1874. This portrait was taken at Taber Studios near the Palace Hotel in San Francisco, before she moved to Washington, D.C. (Courtesy of the Charles Gay collection.)

This is an artist's interpretation of Bird's Nest Glen, where 19th century political and social luminaries met. It was described as a house consisting of two structures—one holding the dining room and kitchen and the other a sitting room and bedrooms, similar to a home Charles knew in Virginia. (Courtesy of the Fairfax Historical Society collection.)

The original Fairfax home is seen here in about 1905, after it had been purchased by the Pastoris and converted to a popular restaurant, which operated from 1893 until it burned in 1911. (Courtesy of the Fairfax Historical Society collection.)

Two California assemblymen, Charles Piercy and Daniel Showalter, fought a duel on May 25, 1861, to settle an insult made over a disagreement on a Union resolution vote. It is said to have been the last political duel fought in California. The duel took place within the area known as Fairfax at that time, but is located within the San Anselmo town limits today. Dr. Thomas Snead, left, and an unidentified friend, right, are listening to John Murray tell of his experiences on the day of the Piercy-Showalter duel. John was a child at the time, living across the creek from the Fairfax estate. He witnessed the principals and friends leave the Fairfax grounds, walking east through the Murray pasture to another clearing near the corner of today's San Anselmo Avenue and Elm Street. When the duel was over, John sneaked down to the field and found blood on the grass where Piercy had fallen and died. John is showing them the approximate location, disproving tales that the duel was fought at Bird's Nest Glen. (Courtesy of the Dr. Thomas Snead collection.)

Four

THE RAILROAD

One of the land transactions made by Manuella Sais in 1875, which would have a profound effect on the upper Ross Valley, was her lease of 1,600 acres to the newly founded North Pacific Coast Railroad. The first train, an inaugural trip from Sausalito to Tomales, would run through the valley and up White's Hill on January 7, 1875. It would forever change the peace and tranquility of a rather pristine terrain. The motivation for building the railroad was to haul timber out of the vast stands of redwoods in Marin and southern Sonoma counties, eventually as far north as Cazadero. Agricultural and dairy products also made up some of the freight shipments.

In addition to freight, the railroad wanted a destination point for passengers. They began to survey the route in February for possible sites and chose the Fairfax area in which to establish a park. By April 1875, they built a covered dancing hall with booths and tables in the shady areas of the new Fairfax Park. The first spring and summer seasons were an overwhelming success with thousands of city folk coming by train every weekend to enjoy the outdoors in Fairfax. The first picnic in April turned wild, with a crowd of 3,000 persons from San Francisco, many of whom were described as "the vilest and most unprincipled of her male and female savages" in attendance. Needless to say, future picnics were heavily patrolled and kept under control, but the reputation established by that first event stayed in memories for a long time.

Organizations throughout the Bay Area scheduled summer weekend picnics in the park via the railroad, a practice that continued for many years. Eventually the railroad turned the running of the picnic grounds over to others, with the property changing owners several times through the years. However, there was no change in its popularity as "the place to go."

In 1902, the North Shore Railroad assumed ownership of the line and made extensive changes and improvements to the system. The NSR bored a new lower tunnel, the Bothin Tunnel, through White's Hill, which shortened the route and eliminated the grueling climb to the upper tunnel. In December 1904, the new tunnel opened. The railroad added a third track to the line as far as Manor, Fairfax's western station, to allow for standard or broad gauge operations in addition to the original narrow gauge cars. The system was electrified as far as Fairfax and fast passenger cars were soon taking Fairfax travelers to Sausalito, where they would then continue on to San Francisco by ferry. High school students from Fairfax would travel by train to Tamalpais High School in Mill Valley via "school special" trains.

In 1907, the line became the Northwestern Pacific Railroad (NWP), with few apparent local changes except for extending electrification from Fairfax to Manor. In 1920, NWP extended the standard gauge track from Manor to Point Reyes Station.

The automobile would soon change travel habits. Rail passenger business dropped off in the 1920s and 1930s and the system was allowed to deteriorate. The completion of the Golden Gate Bridge in 1937 heralded the eventual end of passenger rail travel and buses took over. The last train served Fairfax in February 1941. It had been a good run and most certainly led to the growth of Fairfax as thousands of passengers came, saw the beauty of the area, and chose to stay.

A tranquil scene in 1898, with a steam-powered train arriving at the Fairfax platform before the depot was built, as seen from the highway. Only La Boheme Hotel and Restaurant, center, and Alphonse Bresson's restaurant, left, mark the "downtown" area. (Courtesy of the Newall Snyder collection.)

Engine No. 18 pauses at the Fairfax Station. When built by Brooks Locomotive Works of Dunkirk, New York, and delivered to the North Pacific Coast Railroad in 1899, it was the largest narrow gauge locomotive in the world. It weighed 79,400 pounds and was almost twice the weight of most other engines in the system. It made its last run under NWP ownership in 1929 and was scrapped in 1935. The white building to the left was Rossi's Cafe at the corner of Claus and Sir Francis Drake Boulevard. Today it is the site of a service station. (Courtesy of the Brian Sagar collection.)

A westbound train stops at Pastori Road around 1905 before a station was built. The next stop was Fairfax. Pastori's Hotel and Restaurant is behind the trees, to the right. Cows still graze in the William Murray pasture to the left. (Courtesy of the Fairfax Historical Society collection.)

A Northwestern Pacific Electric train, leaving the Fairfax depot, heads for San Anselmo and Sausalito in the 1930s. (Courtesy of the Fairfax Historical Society collection.)

A View of Fairfax
Station in the distance

Around 1910, this view looks west along the San Rafael-Olema Highway through town. The sign at right advertises the "Fairfax Tavern—Don R. Dunbar, Mgr.," three blocks away at the corner of Bolinas and Park Roads. (Courtesy of the Newall Snyder collection.)

Around 1923, Main Street, left (now Broadway), and the depot are pictured. The smoke above the Alpine Building, on the corner of Bolinas Road, is from barbecues in Fairfax Park. Passengers have just left the train and are heading for the park and picnics, a very common weekend occurrence for many years. (Courtesy of the Fairfax Historical Society collection.)

Pastori, Calif. N.W.P.R.R.

Pastori Station, only a few steps from one of the best restaurants on the West Coast, Pastori's, is seen here off to the left around 1915. The vineyard on the knoll beyond was probably the source of some of the wine that accompanied Pastori's fine cuisine. (Courtesy of the Fairfax Historical Society collection.)

A westbound, narrow gauge freight passes Azalea Avenue at right, Scenic Road in the foreground, and kids (in white) gathered in the park-like setting near Broadway. The redwood arch, at right, was at the entrance to the Fairfax Manor subdivision around 1912. Houses will eventually cover some of the hills beyond. The arch was considered unsafe in 1934 and removed in January 1935. (Courtesy of the Fairfax Historical Society collection.)

The 1875 railroad right-of-way required six trestles to cross small canyons on its steep climb to the tunnel at the summit. This trestle was the highest, shown after abandonment with many ties and supporting beams missing. Kids would sometimes dare each other to walk across the trestle—a risky challenge. (Courtesy of the Fairfax Historical Society collection.)

It has been claimed that the views from the train, as it climbed up the east side of White's Hill, were breathtaking. Passengers would rush to one side of the narrow cars to look down into the canyons below and cause the car to tip. Is this what may have happened here? A work crew was soon on the scene and the cars were pushed upright. No injuries or damage were reported. (Courtesy of the Fairfax Historical Society collection.)

In the 1930s, this electric train sits at Manor Station. The Manor community is off to the right across the bridge. The small building at the lower right is a freight shed. Additional rail sidings, further to the right, allowed trains to be stored here overnight to be ready for morning runs, which took commuters to Sausalito and the ferries. A 1915 trip by train and ferry from Fairfax to the San Francisco Ferry Building took just under an hour, faster than today's bus service. (Courtesy of the Fairfax Historical Society collection.)

Seen here in 1915 is Manor Station and the new bridge, built in 1913, leading to a Manor subdivision. The sign on the roof reads "MANOR elevation 151 feet—to Cazadero 65.53 M—to San Francisco 18.72 M." The original wooden train cars were built as early as 1902 and painted green. They would be supplemented in 1929 with aluminum cars that were painted pumpkin orange. (Courtesy of the Fairfax Historical Society collection.)

The 1904 realignment of the railroad to the new Bothin Tunnel moved the right-of-way to cross Roy Ranch's hay field and this new trestle. Seen here in 1907 are Engines 14 and 33, a double-header, narrow gauge freight train heading west, possibly to Point Reyes Station, Tomales, Occidental, Duncans Mills, and Cazadero. Some of the foundation of the west end of this trestle is still visible on the slope above the basketball courts at White Hill Middle School. (Courtesy of the Fairfax Historical Society collection.)

This photograph was taken by Charles Roy of Vermont, a nephew of John A. Roy, who owned the ranch seen here, the site of today's White Hill School. The trestle across the hay field is faintly visible at the top center. In the foreground, what looks like a dirt road is the original railroad right-of-way that wound its way back into this canyon through a short tunnel below, back out of the canyon, and around the hill to the right. The tracks and ties have been removed, with only a few piles of ties remaining. (Courtesy of the Charles Roy collection.)

Five

THE FAIRFAX PROPERTY
1879–1972

When Ada Fairfax moved to Fort Ross in 1870, she sold Bird's Nest Glen to Mary Owens. Around 1893, Charles Pastori negotiated a lease for the property and started a restaurant at the urging of some of his hunting friends, who proclaimed him to be an excellent chef. He and his friends spent many days hunting in this area, at which times, Pastori would prepare the meals for them. With the help of his wife, Adele, they succeeded in building a reputation for one of the best Italian restaurants on the West Coast—Pastori's.

Charles and Adele Pastori had previously been associated with the theatrical field. Adele was an opera singer and Charles had spent time on the stage as a set builder. Consequently, they both had many friends in the entertainment field, which gave them potential clientele from across the country. Many Broadway, concert, and opera stars were known to have visited them.

When a railroad station was built, just 100 yards from the bridge leading to the property, it was named Pastori. It was an easy trip from San Francisco by ferry and train or horse and buggy. Eventually cars and jitneys would bring patrons onto the grounds for fine food among the beautiful surroundings in the wilds of Marin. The Pastoris were able to buy the property in 1905 and made even more improvements, adding lodging for overnight or extended visits.

In June 1911, Charles Pastori died. Six months later, a fire destroyed the main buildings, which included the home where Charles and Ada Fairfax had lived. Adele vowed to carry on and she immediately started plans to rebuild. By June 1912, Pastori's opened on an even grander scale, with spacious new structures and the tradition of excellence carried on. Adele had four children who supported her efforts to continue. By the mid-1920s, the business climate, compounded by Prohibition, led her to close and sell the property. In 1925, she sold it all to the Emporium, a San Francisco department store, for $250,000, one of the largest real estate transactions in the history of Marin County at that time.

PASTORI'S

PASTORI'S Hotel and Restaurant, Fairfax, Marin County, Calif.

At the south end of Pastori Road, just a few yards from the railroad station, this wooden bridge marked the entrance to Pastori's Hotel and Restaurant. Today's more substantial, concrete bridge replaced the wooden bridge in 1935. (Courtesy of the Newall Snyder collection.)

PASTORI'S Hotel and Restaurant, Fairfax, Marin County, California.

This 1906 postcard shows the outdoor dining area. The people at right center are Adele, Tina (the youngest of the children), and Carlos Pastori. Meals were sometimes served on the tree platform; in fact, at one time a piano was lifted up there and Irving Berlin serenaded guests below. The structure at left is part of the original Fairfax home. (Courtesy of the Brian Sagar collection.)

This is an architect's rendering of the proposed new hotel building to be built on the site of the original Bird's Nest Glen, which was destroyed by fire in 1911. (Courtesy of the Newall Snyder collection.)

The new hotel, with dining rooms and administration offices on the ground floor, is seen shortly after the grand opening. The Pastori family lived in part of the second floor, where some of the guest accommodations were also located. (Courtesy of the Fairfax Historical Society collection.)

The grounds were lavishly landscaped near the main building and the many guest cottages located nearby, as seen in this view from the water tower. Portions of these extensive plantings are still there today. (Courtesy of the Fairfax Historical Society collection.)

This view, from the Pastori apartment on the second floor, looks toward the water tower and one of the rental units. Beyond is an open field, where deer and wild turkeys were often seen and continue to be seen today. (Courtesy of the Fairfax Historical Society collection.)

The Veranda

PASTORI'S   A Bit of Italy in Marin's Gorgeous Hills

Dining in an outdoor setting, such as this covered porch, must have been most pleasant and inspiring. Tina Pastori used to tell of roller-skating for hours in an area like this, after moving the tables and chairs aside. (Courtesy of the Fairfax Historical Society collection.)

The Pastoris were a charitable family who supported many of the local civic functions, donating both time and money. Here Madame Pastori, front center in striped dress, is hosting a gathering of Marin County Red Cross ladies. Tina Pastori is at the rear center, holding a young child. The main building is behind them at right. (Courtesy of the Fairfax Historical Society collection.)

THE EMPORIUM COUNTRY CLUB

The Emporium bought Pastori's in 1925 and turned it into a country club for its many employees. The club was officially dedicated on Sunday, October 11, 1925. Plans were announced for the installation of two swimming pools—one for adults and one for children, a golf course, additional tennis courts, two croquet courts, two baseball diamonds, a handball court, dormitories for men and women, and additional cottages. Many of these features were ready for employee use in the spring of 1926. They planned to have housing accommodations for 600 people. In the early 1930s scene above, tennis courts are at lower right, a covered grandstand is at lower center facing one of the baseball diamonds, and the pool house, just beyond to the left, are all nestled in the sparsely developed hills of Fairfax.

One of the first major improvements made by the Emporium was the construction of the swimming pool in 1927, a feature that would provide much pleasure to several generations of youngsters and grown-ups in the ensuing 47 years, long after the Emporium left the premises. The goal of a second pool never came about under Emporium ownership. The company's 2,000 or so employees, many of whom took advantage of the chance to stay at the "country club," enthusiastically received the club. It soon became the center of social activities for the company. There were dances, departmental sporting competitions, and parties of all kinds, with stock boys and executives alike enjoying the beautiful surroundings. These activities continued until 1937. Enthusiasm apparently diminished as employees found other places to spend leisure times, places where they did not meet their fellow workers so often. The Emporium closed the country club doors to employees in 1937 and leased the property for several years to the Marin School for Boys, a private school, before finally selling in 1943. (Courtesy of the Fairfax Historical Society collection.)

The Emporium inherited the fully landscaped grounds that the Pastoris had so carefully established and maintained over 20 years. The main dining and hotel building are seen here with a carefully manicured lawn—ideal for croquet matches. (Courtesy of the Fairfax Historical Society collection.)

On June 14, 1934, this postcard featuring one of the many guest cottages was sent to a friend in Oakland with part of the message saying, "All we do is swim, play tennis and football and do a little boxing each day and hiked 5 miles." (Courtesy of the Newall Snyder collection.)

In this 1930s image, the vine-covered rear of the main building is seen at right; cottages and service buildings along the creek are seen to the left. The flowing vine had 18 years to develop from the 1912 rebuilding. (Courtesy of the Fairfax Historical Society collection.)

Charlie Fairfax used to fish from his porch overlooking the creek. Apparently when Adele Pastori had the restaurant rebuilt, this feature was retained in the new structure. The Emporium employees might also have enjoyed the same opportunity—fishing before dining. (Courtesy of the Newall Snyder collection.)

MARIN TOWN AND COUNTRY CLUB

San Francisco businessman Max Friedman was looking for a place to pasture his horses. When the Emporium Country Club property became available, this seemed to be an ideal answer for him. He acquired it on November 1, 1943. It had been previously leased to the Marin School for Boys and he permitted such use to continue until the school moved to San Rafael in early 1944. Shortly thereafter, Max realized that the property had the potential for a great recreational facility. On April 23, 1944, the Marin Town and Country Club opened to the public and became an immediate success, with 1,500 in attendance for the opening day. The turnout exceeded Max's wildest dreams. A smiling attendant greeted those who entered the grounds and accepted the money for a day of entertainment—swimming, picnicking, athletic events, or just lounging around in the beautiful surroundings.

That first year Max sponsored a baseball team, the Fairfax Boys Athletic Club, which soon became a training ground for players, some of whom went on to become professionals for teams such as the New York Yankees. An avid sports fan, he also sponsored a basketball team for many years. Improvements were made during the first few years for the benefit of the public. Several more pools were added, including a diving pool and wading pools. Eventually there were seven pools in all. Volleyball and basketball courts, enlarged picnic area (including barbecue pits), children's play equipment, and an expanded lawn area for sunbathing were added. A cafeteria, a snack bar complete with a jukebox, and a first-class restaurant with a bar, serving lunch and dinner under the guidance of "Famous San Francisco Chef Maldi" and a staff of eight, provided excellent fare for the guests. (Courtesy of the Fairfax Historical Society collection)

The 1946 season brought the gala opening of an outdoor dance floor, the Redwood Bowl, which became immensely popular every Saturday night. The music even went out over the airwaves with a half-hour broadcast on San Francisco radio station KYA. Nationally known big bands, playing in hotels in San Francisco, would often travel to Fairfax to provide the music for these dances. During the day, the dance floor was sometimes used for beauty contests, open to all, with prizes to the winning contestants. Schools, churches, corporations, and many other organized groups would schedule the use of the entire facility for a weekend. Crowds as large as 5,000 would sometimes attend. When smaller organizations would reserve a day, Max would assign each group a specific area in which to assemble. The Marin Town and Country Club became well known around the Bay Area and beyond. Max's right-hand man was Guido Monte, hired as the club manager at the beginning of the second season. "Monte," as all knew him, was in charge of hiring the staff needed to keep things running smoothly. The season ran from April 15 to the end of September and afforded many students a chance for summer employment. Many local residents recall times spent as lifeguards at the pools, pool house attendants, waiters, bartenders, or at other jobs around the club—the first job for many. Off-duty law enforcement officers were often hired as security personnel. Over the 28 years of operation, the club maintained a reputation as a well-run, disciplined operation until it closed in 1972. Max and Monte saw to that. In the photograph above, Max Friedman, left, and Guido Monte stand in front of the sign that helped make the place so popular. There were 40 of these signs scattered around the Bay Area, stating, "When it's cold and foggy in San Francisco—it's like THIS over here." (Courtesy of the Fairfax Historical Society collection.)

A 1953 aerial view shows Max's former horse corral being used as a parking lot on a moderately busy day. Baseball diamonds are at each end of the corral. The diving pool has been added, left center, with basketball courts and the main pool above them. The administration/restaurant building is at top center. (Courtesy of the Fairfax Historical Society collection.)

This 1956 aerial view from over downtown Fairfax shows the corral gone and another pool in its place. The connector between Center Boulevard, the old railroad right-of-way, and Broadway in downtown would be built in 1958. In 1960, Fair Anselm Shopping Center was built on part of Max Friedman's property. The Fairfax Theater, lower center, had opened on June 30, 1950—six years previously. (Courtesy of the Fairfax Historical Society collection.)

Saturday night dances, held under the stars in the Redwood Bowl, featured a 10-piece orchestra and were a popular summer event. The dances look rather formal by today's standards. Starting in 1946, KYA radio broadcast the music of these dances on a live half-hour program. Below, Bill Clifford, playing trombone, stands with Max Friedman. Bill Clifford and Orchestra were hired to play at the Redwood Bowl for the 1947 season. Other well-known bands such as Skinnay Ennis and Noel Thomas would also provide music over the years. Max made every effort to please his patrons and provide wholesome entertainment. (Courtesy of the Friedman family collection.)

The pool was the main attraction for many, including San Franciscans who came seeking warmer weather during the summer. It also provided a good place for girl- and boy-watching among the predominant younger crowd. (Courtesy of the Friedman family collection.)

For the more adventurous or experienced guests, the diving pool provided a chance to show one's ability. (Courtesy of the Friedman family collection.)

There were great expanses of lawn area for sunbathing, providing ample opportunity for deep tans (before concerns about ultraviolet rays). It took a staff of 80 to keep the daily operations running smoothly and the grounds well maintained. (Courtesy of the Friedman family collection.)

If a family didn't bring its own picnic food to barbecue in the available pits, the cafeteria offered hamburgers, hot dogs, and beverages. The Dinning Room was a popular hangout for teenagers. (Courtesy of the Friedman family collection.)

Six

DOWNTOWN
BUSINESS AND PEOPLE

Since Fairfax includes many hills, it is only natural that the lower parts of the town—the valleys—should be considered the downtown area. It was in this area that the first development took place after the railroad's initial venture through the valley in 1875, beginning with a platform to accommodate the many passengers getting off the train to visit the park the railroad had established. Merchants later built in the area, seeking to satisfy the passengers' need for food and drink beyond what they might bring as picnickers.

The first known commercial structure to be built outside the park was the Fairfax House, a roadhouse or saloon established by Alphonse Bresson. He was the brother of Joseph, who had married Dominga Sais, and ran their 700-acre farm west of the downtown area. As early as 1889, the Fairfax House was open for business on the south side of the tracks. Around 1900, another saloon, the Fairfax Park Annex, would appear across Bolinas Road. A third building followed when Alphonse relocated his business to the other side of the tracks.

One by one, new buildings and merchants appeared, as businessmen moved in to benefit from the growing population resulting from the visitors who had become permanent residents. The railroad operators had promoted travel to Fairfax Park from the very first summer of operation in 1875, and as an additional source of income for the railroad. It was common for thousands to attend picnics in the park, as many organizations in San Francisco scheduled their annual outings here so that members could enjoy a day in the country among the redwoods. It was a welcome and unique change from city life. Many of the weekend visitors enjoyed the beauty of the area and decided this would be a good place to live, so they moved in permanently.

In the following photographs, you will see the growth of the business sector of Fairfax, and some of the adjacent residential areas, meet some of the people involved, and enjoy a few miscellaneous views of life in early Fairfax.

Company M, 1st Cavalry, which numbered 70 men, camped out in Fairfax in August 1883 for two months. Their encampment area was bounded by Inyo, Mono, Pacheco, and the north end of Dominga Avenue. The dark line running across the photograph is a line of about 70 horses, with several cannons just beyond them. With some magnification, one can see the flagpole on the Fairfax Park grounds, part of the rear of La Boheme, and the front of Alphonse Bresson's restaurant across the highway. This is one of the earliest non-studio photographs. (Courtesy of the Fairfax Historical Society collection.)

A 1889 sketch by Mill Valley artist Charles Ehrer shows the 1884 Fairfax House, the train platform, and the Fairfax Park Pavilion buried in the trees at upper left. Just above center is the flagpole visible from the cavalry grounds. The park extended from the corner of the road leading around to the right of Fairfax House, back into the trees, and beyond Park Road. The San Rafael-Olema Highway is in the foreground near the happily grazing California cows. (Courtesy of the Marin County Historical Society collection.)

This *c.* 1915 view is similar to the previous sketch, only it's some 25 years later looking down on the Fairfax Park Annex. It shows an entrance to the park with a path leading up to the grass area and the flagpole. Picnic tables were located among the trees beyond. Thousands of people would flock here on weekends. (Courtesy of the Newall Snyder collection.)

La Boheme Hotel and Restaurant, left, replaced the Fairfax House. The Fairfax Park Annex, right, a former saloon, was on the corner of Bolinas Road and Main Street, marking a corner of Fairfax Park. The annex was built around 1900 by Martin Petersen as his home. In 1893, he had bought the park. The very small building in between is a real estate office, offering lots in the Deer Park subdivision, which came on the market in 1914. (Courtesy of the Newall Snyder collection.)

This view looks up Main Street, around 1908, from near the railroad platform. The La Boheme Hotel and Restaurant is at the left and the Fairfax Park Annex beyond. The lone oak tree in the distance is on park grounds. (Courtesy of the Fairfax Historical Society collection.)

This photograph looks east along Main Street (today's Broadway) in 1908, with the railroad platform at left. The Fairfax Park Annex building, right, had an apartment at the near end where the Henry Frustuck family lived after they moved here from San Francisco and bought Fairfax Park in 1905. It later became Henry's real estate office. (Courtesy of the Fairfax Historical Society collection.)

Around 1907, some of the local kids in town are pictured on Main Street in front of La Boheme. They are Caesar Balangero, Tina Pastori, Madeline Balangero, Ione Pastori (on horse), and Marguerite Balangero. The Balangeros owned La Boheme, and Tina and Ione's parents owned Pastori's several blocks away. The fact that their parents were business competitors didn't keep them from enjoying each others company. (Courtesy of the Fairfax Historical Society collection.)

A 1912 eastbound train heading for Sausalito has just arrived at the station and the new depot building. Adding windows in the openings on three sides solved complaints about exposure during stormy weather. On the distant Manor Hill, the path has been cleared for the incline railroad, which began running in August 1913. The sign on the depot reads "FAIRFAX elevation 116 feet To San Francisco 17.74 M To Cazadero 68.19 M." (Courtesy of Newall Snyder collection.)

Regular La Boheme customers seen here, from left to right, are Mr. and Mrs. Laviosa, Anetta Qualia, and Mr. and Mrs. Garbe. Anetta was the daughter of one of the co-owners of the resort. The Laviosas of San Rafael had dinner at La Boheme every Sunday, as did the Garbes of San Francisco. The redwood grove of about 20 trees was where 19 Broadway is today. Only two or three of these trees still stand. (Courtesy of the Fairfax Historical Society collection.)

On the grounds of La Boheme, behind the building on Main Street, are Theresa Balangero and her daughters Marguerite and Madeline. In 1915, La Boheme served a dinner for 35¢, with claims "to have no equal for the price." (Courtesy of the Fairfax Historical Society collection.)

La Boheme had new neighbors in 1912—a real estate office on the far side and a grocery/cigar store whose sign advertises "Gasoline 25 cents per gal." In the early years of the horseless carriage, it was common for grocers to carry fuel for the occasional vehicle that might venture this far, especially since there was no garage or service station in town during the early 1910s. (Courtesy of the Newall Snyder collection.)

In November 1915, La Boheme and the adjacent Croker Building along Bolinas Road burned down. They were replaced, in part, by these structures at 23 and 25 Broadway, which still stand today. The far building, a real estate office, advertises "R. A. Carey & Co. The Cascades," properties which were promoted from 1914 through 1926. This building exists today as Cafe Amsterdam. The building that housed the E. Allora Grill/Restaurant has also passed through several owners, and uses. It is now the Siam Lotus Thai restaurant. (Courtesy of the D. Olsen collection.)

When the Golden Gate Bridge opened in May 1937, the railroads suffered an even greater loss of passengers. When the last train ran on February 28, 1941, 25 Broadway became the Greyhound bus depot. Some alterations have been made to the front of the building. (Courtesy of the Newall Snyder collection.)

Nella Celoni stands in front of the family's Celoni's Grill and Restaurant around 1930. The right half of the building, at 19 Broadway, was built as the Fairfax Hotel and Restaurant in November 1921 by Albert Balangero. He built the other half, 17 Broadway, a year later. The Celonis acquired the property sometime around 1929. (Courtesy of the Celoni collection.)

The western third of the Park Annex building became the real estate office of Frustuck and Wreden, developers of the Fairfax Park subdivision. In 1911, Bill and Fred Bridges await potential buyers on a summer afternoon. The building was razed in 1919 to make way for Frank Healion's Alpine Building. (Courtesy of the Newall Snyder collection.)

In 1912, the Park Annex lost its liquor license and became the Fairfax Park Coffee and Lunch House, still owned by Henry Frustuck. He is the gent in the vest, standing by the car behind the bush. A sign, "Free Ride to Cascades," refers to the car parked at the curb, which would take interested persons to the Cascades subdivision about half a mile up Bolinas Road. Henry Frustuck owned Fairfax Park from 1905 to 1920. (Courtesy of the Newall Snyder collection.)

In 1920, the Alpine Building, center, opened at a total cost of $24,000. It housed a grocery, soda fountain, meat market, tailor, and shoe repair on the ground floor and a library and doctors' offices on the second floor. In 1917, C. Grosjean and Company Grocers took over the former Blagg and Son space in the new Croker Building, left. Grosjean was Marin's first chain grocery store with additional stores located in San Rafael, San Anselmo, and Lagunitas. Today it is Fradelezio's Restaurant. (Courtesy of the Newall Snyder collection.)

In the early 1930s, the Alpine building was an impressive structure. In 1936, owner Frank Healion built a two-story addition on the Broadway side which housed the library for a number of years on the ground level. A physician and surgeon, Dr. Osborn; a dentist, Dr. Rutner; and a beauty parlor were upstairs. Signs indicate coffee sold for 24¢ a pound, bacon at 19¢ per pound, and corn flakes for 8¢ a box—all bargains today. (Courtesy of the Charles Grasso collection.)

Frank Healion and Catherine McKay were married on May 2, 1918, and lived in the Cascades for many years before moving to San Rafael, where he pursued a career in real estate. At the age of 19, Frank took the 1910 census on horseback, covering the county north and west of San Rafael. In 1910, there was a county population of only 1,000. (Courtesy of the Frank Healion collection.)

Frank Healion was proud of his 12-stool soda fountain and spent much of his time there dispensing sodas, sundaes, and ice cream cones. The store was especially busy on weekends when the picnickers would pass by on their way from the trains to the park. He would hire local youth to help out at the fountain. The other fellow pictured is Clyde Smith, head of the grocery department. (Courtesy of the Fairfax Historical Society collection.)

On Broadway, *c.* 1922, Blagg Brothers, a tea and coffee shop, and York's Hardware were located in what are today's Koffee Klatch and Fairfax Variety. Those are probably proprietors and friends posing with the traditional delivery truck. Increased construction work in the area spurred the building of supply stores in town and, in 1920, a scarcity of nails actually slowed new construction for a while. (Courtesy of the Fairfax Historical Society collection.)

This *c.* 1922 view gives one a closer look at P. J. Boscus Hardware and Plumbing at 65 Broadway and Brooks and Blank, grocers at 67 Broadway. The sign on the roof indicates that 71 Broadway is Fairfax Park Coffee and Lunch House, probably relocated when their building was torn down to make way for the Alpine Building (not pictured) down the street. Home deliveries were an important part of doing business in those times. (Courtesy of the Newall Snyder collection.)

This 1935 view taken near the bank looks down Broadway. Fairfax Park Coffee and Lunch House has become the Alpine Restaurant. The 1930 Buick parked near the bank attests to the casual driving habits of the time. The west side addition has not yet been added to the Alpine Building. (Courtesy of the Brian Sagar collection.)

In December 1921, the Fairfax Bank was dedicated. In September 1925, it became the Bank of Italy, and later, Bank of America. The oak tree stands on Fairfax Park property, not far from Main Street. It was removed when the present bank was built in the late 1950s and the original bank building was demolished. (Courtesy of the Newall Snyder collection.)

When Fairfax Manor lots came on the market in 1913, a redwood log arch was built as a gateway to the subdivision. It was declared unsafe and taken down in the early 1930s. Just above the corner office sign, on the roof, a white horse shares a yard with a family—real country living. Under the arch is a tent cabin, temporary living quarters for the Miller family, who bought a lot in the vicinity of 9 Scenic Road. (Courtesy of the Fairfax Historical Society collection.)

"Tent in Fairfax Manor" was written below this photograph, with the same tent as seen in the previous photograph. Nothing fancy, it was adequate for camping out in Fairfax's ideal summer climate. The kids enjoy the luxury of a porch. Many summer homes in Fairfax started this way. (Courtesy of the C. E. Miller collection.)

Pictured in the 1920s are the Fairfax Lumber Company, left, and Fairfax School. The lumber company started as Hanson and Gordon Lumber Company in 1913 and, on January 1, 1915, became Fairfax Lumber Company, offering millwork, cabinetwork, hardware, and building supplies to meet the needs of a growing community. It is the oldest remaining business in town. The original mill building is still located within the present structure. (Courtesy of the Fairfax Historical Society collection.)

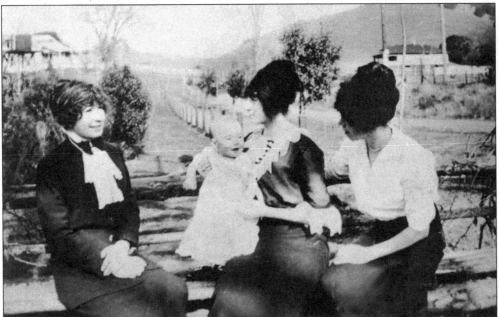

At the end of Broadway was another resort, Buon Gusto Villa, which started as a restaurant before the beginning of the 20th century. Angelo Grasso purchased the business in 1913. Some of his family members, shown above from left to right, are Ethel, baby Russell, Elva, and Elizabeth Grasso. Part of the villa can be seen in the upper left corner of the photograph. The Grasso family ran the resort until 1919 and then sold it to Fiori Giannini. It closed in 1962. The property was sold in 1965 for construction of the Fairfax Library. (Courtesy of the Charles Grasso collection.)

This c. 1920 view, taken from Bolinas Road, looks across Broadway to the train station. The station now has windows. Fairfax Heights is developing on the hill beyond and the Croker Building, right, obviously has a barber as a tenant—a barber pole the size of a gasoline pump stands at the curb. Through 1950, a barbershop would be in business at 3 Bolinas Road. (Courtesy of the Newall Snyder collection.)

An early 1920s view shows Bolinas Road and businesses in the new Croker Building. The first Croker structure burned in 1915 and was immediately rebuilt. It survives today with new tenants. People have left the depot and are heading up the street to Fairfax Park, on the right. Note the open space along the way. It was soon developed. (Courtesy of the Newall Snyder collection.)

In 1924, the Fairfax Market was established by the Fong brothers, Harry and Tom, next to the Alpine Building. Tom is behind their delivery wagon, which was typical of every grocery store in town. (Courtesy of the Tom Fong collection.)

Inside the Fairfax Market are two clerks with Tom Fong, nearest the front counter. It was a very neat and well-stocked establishment, in business until 1984. Fairfax was the first town in the county where stores would be open on Sunday to benefit from the crowds of weekend visitors. (Courtesy of the Tom Fong collection.)

Paul Nave came to Fairfax in 1920 and built this building in 1924. He and his family lived upstairs and he ran a produce market in half of the store while George Coco ran a meat market in the other half. In 1935, Paul closed the store and converted it to the bar that exists today at 24 Bolinas Road. (Courtesy of the Fairfax Historical Society collection.)

In November 1928, A. Luchesi and E. Capestri opened the Marin Ravioli and Tagliarini Factory in the Croker Building at 15 Bolinas Road. This was the same year that the Dundases vacated the space next door and moved across the street to their new pharmacy. In 1938, Jerry and Babe Cervelli opened Jerry's Food Center, a meat and grocery store, in the former Dundas space at 17 Bolinas Road. (Courtesy of the Fairfax Historical Society collection.)

William and Pauline Dundas are seen here in front of their first drug store in town. Both pharmacists, they took over the L. S. Whitaker Pharmacy in the Croker Building in 1925. Three years later, they built a new building across the street at 28 Bolinas Road. (Courtesy of the Newall Snyder collection.)

In the 1930s, UC engineering students had a field camp at Sky Oaks above Fairfax. The students would arrive by train and await transport to the camp. Here five of them are greeted by some Fairfax lasses and William Dundas, second from right in the front row. Geraldine Johnson is next to him and Marguerite Grandjean is directly behind her. Both young ladies worked for Dundas at his soda fountain across the street. The building at 31 Bolinas Road became Cartamo's Acme Garage. (Courtesy of the Fairfax Historical Society collection.)

In December 1928, the new Dundas Pharmacy, built at 28 Bolinas Road, opened. The store became well known for its outstanding artistic window displays. Dundas had spacious living quarters in the rear of the building. They sold to Pilson's Pharmacy in 1939 and it remained a pharmacy until the mid-1950s. It became a shoe store in the 1970s, then a bike store, and is now a bookstore, Book Beat. (Courtesy of the Newall Snyder collection.)

In April 1930, Dundas Pharmacy inaugurated a new soda fountain, seen here covered with Easter baskets. Marguerite Grandjean had first worked at Frank Healion's soda fountain in the Alpine Building at the other end of the block, but was enticed by a raise in salary to work for Dundas. Both fountains probably did very well catering to the picnic crowds since they were located on the way from the train to Fairfax Park. (Courtesy of the Newall Snyder collection.)

The northwest corner of Park and Bolinas Road Roads saw many owners over the years. The Fairfax Tavern, which was built in 1906 by Madame Caramelli, is shown in the 1930s. Lena Rossi owned it from 1919 to 1946. Don Dunbar was manager during part of that time, when it was also known as the Dunbar Hotel. There were a few rental cabins scattered on the hill and in the woods nearby. (Courtesy of D. Olsen collection.)

The Hamilton House is pictured toward the end of its days. In 1955, the building was torn down and replaced with hillside apartments and a Richfield service station, followed later by a 7-Eleven store, at street level. Another landmark gone. (Courtesy of the Brian Sagar collection.)

This c. 1915 view looks down at the junctions of Cascade Drive, Cypress Drive, and Hickory Road before much construction had taken place. One of the two oak trees still stands at One Hickory Road. The Frustuck house is at the lower right, overlooking this scene. Kenneth "Doc" Edgar Park, with its redwood trees, is in the triangular plot in front of the twin oaks at the entrance to The Cascades. (Courtesy of the Frustuck-Sanborn collection.)

In the kitchen at Deer Park Villa in 1946 are Edna Croce, John Brojello, Antoinette Ghiringhelli, Enrico Croce, and Joseph Ghiringhelli. Deer Park Villa, under the ownership of Joe Ghiringhelli, opened in December 1937 and is Fairfax's oldest restaurant, offering excellent Italian cuisine. Enrico Croce opened his own restaurant downtown around 1960 and called it Enrico's. It now houses Fradelezio's Restaurant at 35 Broadway. (Courtesy of the Ghiringhelli collection.)

In the 1920s, a surrey with fringe on top is parked in the woods of the Deer Park area. This may have been the "taxi" for the photographer capturing the wilderness of that part of town before its development. (Courtesy of the Newall Snyder collection.)

In 1920, the Marin County supervisors promised to start sprinkling the roads of Fairfax with a water cart "as soon as one became available." Apparently they followed through and Harry Hansen pauses along Sir Francis Drake Boulevard during sprinkling operations, not far from the Fairfax Garage and Blagg's store. (Courtesy of the Marin County Historical Society collection.)

This house, at 1571 Sir Francis Drake Boulevard, originally had a saloon in the front half of the first floor. It was 100 feet east, in San Anselmo. When San Anselmo went dry in 1907, forbidding alcohol sales, owner Dominic Arbini moved his house 100 feet west into Fairfax to stay in business. Some years later, he built the Ole Timer's Tavern next door to move the saloon out of his dwelling. Both are there today. Steel rings for tying up a horse still exist in the front wall of the house and the former tavern. (Courtesy of the Fairfax Historical Society collection.)

Inside the Ole Timer's Tavern, around 1915, several patrons are lined up at the bar. The bar is still in place, but the business has changed several times. It is now a beauty bar. (Courtesy of the Becky Soldavini collection.)

In the early 1930s, De Maestri's City Limit Garage was also at the east end of town. Babe De Maestri and Dick Keating are standing near the gas pumps. In 1963, De Maestri bought and moved into the Fairfax Garage at 1812 Sir Francis Drake Boulevard, where it is still in business today. (Courtesy of the Ed De Maestri collection.)

An early 1920s view looks east along Sir Francis Drake Boulevard. To the far left at the top is the Ole Timer's Tavern; at lower right is Reception, another roadside restaurant and bar, now Pancho Villa's Restaurant. Another tavern, which burned down in 1927, is seen at bottom center. (Courtesy of the Fairfax Historical Society collection.)

In the 1890s, Camille Grosjean leased 50 acres up the valley along Willow Street, planting a vineyard, as seen above. This was somewhat typical of many of the hills around Fairfax, where wine was an essential beverage. Camille sold the property to developers in 1905 and, in 1907, it became the Ridgeway Park subdivision, the first residential subdivision in Fairfax. (Courtesy of the Fairfax Historical Society collection.)

Greatly enlarged, the Rossi's Hotel, Cafe, and Grill, seen here around 1912, was built up to the road. The original building is visible to the right behind the white picket fence. (Courtesy of the D. Olsen collection.)

In 1905, J. J. Blagg leased some of the Bresson property along Sir Francis Drake Boulevard and a year later built his Hillside Tavern. In early 1910, Mr. Blagg initiated a request of the U.S. government to start a post office in the area. The government was quick to respond, and by June 8, the Fairfax Post Office was established in Blagg's store. He became the town's first postmaster as well as the first mayor in 1931. He is standing in front of his tavern, next to one of the hitching posts. (Courtesy of the Fairfax Historical Society collection.)

By 1918, other buildings had been built next to Blagg's, including a barbershop and a new post office, built in 1915. In 1929, these buildings were torn down to make way for a service station, which remained in business through 1950. Apartments now occupy the site. (Courtesy of the Newall Snyder collection.)

In 1916, the Fairfax Garage was built by the Rocca Brothers, developers of the Fairfax Heights subdivision. Shown at left in 1917 is Ermengildo Pordon, an early owner of Fairfax Garage, possibly the first. Pordon also owned a dealership for Reo automobiles, a car built from 1904 to 1936 by Ransom E. Olds and named for his initials, R. E. O. (Courtesy of the Ed De Maestri collection.)

The garage changed ownership many times over the years. One of its owners was M. Williams, who still ran the Reo dealership, as shown. Fairfax finally had its first gasoline pump and service station. (Courtesy of the Newall Snyder collection.)

This horse appears dejected, perhaps as it realizes that the automobile is taking over its primary purpose in life. M. Williams is still proprietor of the Fairfax Garage, but it is now selling Durant Cars, built from 1921 to 1932. This scene was taken around 1924 as Frank Healion buys a Star car, an automobile built by a branch of Durant Motors. (Courtesy of the Fairfax Historical Society collection.)

In 1914, Maple Hall was completed on the corner of Taylor and Sir Francis Drake Boulevard. In 1915, the concrete sidewalk is being poured for another block westward. Rocca Brothers occupies the corner space. Holweg's Drug store and a pool room are next door. The top floor became a valuable assembly and auditorium space for movies, dances, and meetings. A fire in early 1921 destroyed this top floor, but the first floor spaces were salvaged and repaired and are still occupied today. (Courtesy of the Fairfax Historical Society collection.)

A few doors further west along Sir Francis Drake Boulevard, in late 1921, M. Linggi has just completed his new two-story building, with apartments upstairs and cabinet/carpentry shop on the ground floor. The post office and Rocca Brothers real estate office have moved to the near building. Just next to the power pole is Maple Hall, which is missing the top story from the previously mentioned fire. (Courtesy of the Newall Snyder collection.)

Around 1915, Julia Arbini, center, and two friends stand in front of the post office, where Julia would be postmaster until 1937. This location for the post office opened in 1915 and it would remain here for 34 years. (Courtesy of the Arbini family collection.)

In September 1949, the Fairfax Post Office moved into this building at 1916 Sir Francis Drake Boulevard, specifically built to serve its needs and just two doors from its previous location. This location would serve until 1978 when the post office moved to the present building. Perry's Delicatessen now occupies this building. (Courtesy of the Fairfax Historical Society collection.)

Nelson and Carol Gamas, Viola and Jim Wolverton, and an unidentified child are in front of Gamas Shell Service Station at the corner of Claus Circle and Sir Francis Drake Boulevard around 1948. Nelson, who ran this station from 1945 to 1953, was a neighbor of Dr. Thomas Snead. (Courtesy of the Fairfax Historical Society collection.)

In 1939, Dr. Snead built and began his dental practice in this unique office, unusual in that few dentists had their own buildings and most, even today, occupy shared buildings. At that time, it was one of two dental buildings in the county. Dr. Snead practiced here for 50 years, retiring in 1989. He had moved to Fairfax with his parents as a youth and grew up here, commuting to San Francisco for his medical education. (Courtesy of the Dr. Thomas Snead collection.)

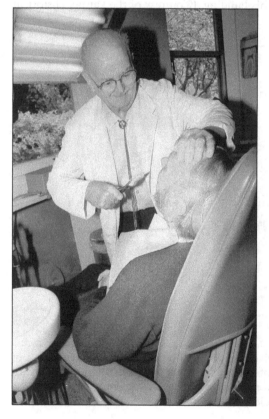

In 1989, Dr. Snead demonstrates his extraction procedure on Bill Allen during a farewell visit to his office. "Open wide, this won't hurt a bit," was a refrain heard often, but no teeth were actually pulled at this appointment. (Courtesy of the Fairfax Historical Society collection.)

On February 22, 1901, a group of hikers, members of the Marin County Association of Tramps and Wanderers, Ltd., made one of their frequent trips to Fairfax, via the train, to hike in the nearby hills. Arthur Jordan is setting up a Pocket Kodak to take their picture. Across the highway is the former Alphonse Bresson's restaurant, later named Rossi's Cafe. Note the vineyard on the hill at left. (Courtesy of the Sausalito Historical Society collection.)

Here is the photograph that Arthur took—a fine looking bunch of hikers in typical outdoor wear, ready to start their hike. Apparently hats were mandatory, even a derby. Arthur even got in the picture, the gentleman in the center with leggings. At left is part of the Fairfax Park Annex, the saloon at the corner of Fairfax Park. (Courtesy of the Sausalito Historical Society collection.)

The Fairfax Owls are holding a banquet on April 24, 1915, at Rossi's Cafe. Attendees, from left to right, are the following: unidentified, Frank Valentine, Roy Brown, Sid Eschen, Bill Wilson, unidentified, Mr. Campbell, Ed Jory, Charlie Bolte, Clyde Griffin, Ed Rossi, Sid Pollard, Earl ?, Fred ?, James Rossi, Mary Piantinida, Fred Miles, Henry Dilges, and Sam Hayes. Unfortunately the Rossi buildings burned down November 13, 1929, and would be replaced by a miniature golf course in August 1930. Rino gas station is located there today. (Courtesy of the Fairfax Historical Society collection.)

In 1897, John A. Roy bought this ranch, the site of today's White Hill School. In 1904, the Healions leased the property and Frank Healion, age 16, was living here in 1907 when this photograph was taken. They managed a sizeable herd of dairy cattle and it was Frank's job to take the milk to market everyday. (Courtesy of the Fairfax Historical Society collection.)

This view looks east from the Roy pasture, today's Lefty Gomez Field, toward Fairfax, with some of the dairy herd grazing nearby. The San Rafael-Olema Highway is beyond the trees to the right. (Courtesy of the Charles Roy collection.)

The 1907 hay harvest takes place on the Roy Ranch, during the time the Healions were leasing the property. (Courtesy the Charles Roy collection.)

The spacious new Roy home, where John Roy would retire, was a quarter mile east of the original farm buildings. This home, on Glen Drive, was destroyed in 1973 to make way for residential development. The Roy family members came from Vermont and first settled in the San Geronimo Valley, a few miles west of Fairfax. In the early 1900s, John Roy bought the Fairfax farm property and moved in. He leased it to others when he retired. (Courtesy the Charles Roy collection.)

On the porch of the Roy home in 1907, from left to right, are (first row) owners Barbara and John Roy; (second row) Charles Roy, their nephew visiting from Vermont, and three unidentified women. John Roy had retired and was enjoying a life of leisure. (Courtesy the Charles Roy collection.)

In 1875, the railroad established Fairfax Park during its first year of operation, creating a very popular destination point for picnickers and seekers of fun and games. The original 1,500 acres were quickly reduced to 63 and finally to around 9 acres, still maintaining some of the wooded charm of the original. It was fenced in 1920, when purchased by the Volunteer Fire Department, to ensure sales for paid events on weekends. It was open to the public during the week. (Courtesy of the Fairfax Historical Society collection.)

This is a 1911 view of an entrance to Fairfax Park from Main Street, now Broadway. There were 63 acres in which to roam, play, and picnic. Henry Frustuck and Henry Wreden had built "the largest enclosed pavilion on the West Coast" in 1908, partly visible in the trees at upper left. In 1921, it was replaced by the present pavilion. The lone oak tree would survive in the business part of town until the late 1950s. (Courtesy of the Newall Snyder collection.)

In the 1920s, a small portion of the picnic grounds could be seen among the redwoods. The grounds are still evident, but to a lesser extent today. (Courtesy of the Fairfax Historical Society collection.)

In the 1920s, a merry-go-round with a canvas top would be moved in during the summer season for entertainment. It was owned and run by a private party. (Courtesy of the Fairfax Historical Society collection.)

The pavilion, built in 1921 by the Fairfax Volunteer Fire Department, has served the community well for the past 85 years. It was built at an appropriate time, just after the fire at Maple Hall destroyed the town's major assembly hall. It has served as a locale for dances, lectures, movies, a skating rink, concerts (Nelson Eddy sang here in 1934), and many other functions requiring a large indoor space in town. (Courtesy of the Newall Snyder collection.)

A rare, early interior view of the pavilion shows it decorated for a special occasion, possibly the traditional Fourth of July festivities. (Courtesy of the Newall Snyder collection.)

"Barbecue of the Portuguese Convention at Fairfax, Marin Co, Cal. Sept. 17, 1908" is the title of this occasion in the park, typical of the many organizations from San Francisco, and other cities around the Bay Area, who would reserve the park for a day and fill it with thousands of pleasure-seeking members. Bread for everyone! (Courtesy of the Newall Snyder collection.)

The Fairfax Volunteer Fire Department was proud of their new Seagrave fire truck when it was delivered in 1929, the first town of its size to have one of these "modern pumpers." The town still has this truck and brings it out on special occasions, such as when Charles Fairfax's great-great nephew Hon. Hugh Fairfax and his family visited in August 2002. (Courtesy of the Fairfax Historical Society collection.)

In 1926, a new fire station was built and dedicated in February 1927. The town hall will be built adjacent in 1940 to accommodate the police department, town clerk, and other departments. (Courtesy of the Newall Snyder collection.)

In 1911, the Fairfax Volunteer Fire Department began and was considered one of the best in the country. Posing here in the late 1920s, from left to right, are (first row) Silvio Piffero, Primo Testa, Chief Joseph Capelli, John Hicks, and Melvin Martini; (second row) Ned Ongaro, Frank Harrison, Henry Vonderheide, Leo Nusbaum, Bob Harrigan, and Frank Johnson. (Courtesy of the Fairfax Historical Society collection.)

At the October 1919 meeting of the Fairfax Fire Commission, it was decided to relocate and paint this hose reel enclosure on Bolinas Road. It cost $50 to move and paint it. Its new location was on the west side of Pastori Avenue in what is today Albertson's Market parking lot. In case of a nearby fire, several volunteer firemen would pull out the cart, roll it to the fire and the nearest fireplug, make the necessary connections, and douse the flames. There were several of these small firehouses scattered around town. (Courtesy of the Fairfax Historical Society collection.)

Constable Andrew Peri is on the motorcycle around 1926 with the Fairfax Park Police. Second from left is Leo Tracy and third from right is Horst Carter. Andrew Peri's career began in 1924 when he was appointed as the town's night watchman, working seven days a week from 9:00 p.m. to dawn. In 1927, he was appointed as the first Fairfax police officer and, when the town was incorporated in 1931, became chief of police at age 27, the youngest chief in the state. (Courtesy of the Peri family collection.)

In 1939, police chief Andrew Peri proudly shows off the town's new Studebaker police car in front of the firehouse. Andy was greatly admired by the townspeople. Honoring his great concern for the town's youth, the children's playground on Park Road was named for him as a tribute to his 31 years of service. (Courtesy of the Peri family collection.)

Five of Fairfax's finest line up in front of town hall in the 1950s. Pictured here, from left to right, are Cliff Cordes, Manuel Azevido, Chief Andrew Peri, Norman Christensen, and Henry Vonderheide. Cliff Cordes joined the Fairfax Police force at the age of 50 in 1944 and became the town's second chief of police upon the death of Andy Peri in 1959. When he retired in 1962, he was succeeded by Chief Chuck Grasso. (Courtesy of the Fairfax Historical Society collection.)

The Honor Grove, in the park along Bolinas Road, was established in 1944 to honor the servicemen from Fairfax who served in World War II. Six plaques were mounted on redwoods, listing the names and branch of service of each Fairfax resident serving in the military. Weather and vandalism eventually took their toll and they were removed and put into storage. A new stone monument and brass plaque were built on this same site in 1991, when the grove was rededicated. (Courtesy of the Newall Snyder collection.)

In 1915, the Manor Post Office opened for business to serve what was intended to be the new Town of Manor, but the area was eventually absorbed into the city limits of Fairfax. The post office closed on December 31, 1953, and is now a private home with a second story addition. (Courtesy of the Fairfax Historical Society collection.)

This white structure, seen in West Fairfax around 1912, is the greenhouse of Nivens Nursery, which would later move to Larkspur. The Olema Highway runs down to the left. Buon Gusto Villa is on the knoll at the center among the trees, today's library site. St. Rita's Church will be built across the highway from Buon Gusto in 1916, next to the two homes. To the right of the greenhouse is a barn housing the Manor Hill water system. (Courtesy of the Fairfax Historical Society collection.)

Buying a lot on Manor Hill sometimes meant camping out on the property until the house was built, with the developer providing canvas for the tent. Along with his parents, 12-year-old Tom Snead camped out one summer on the lot they had purchased on Ridge Road. There was water, but no electricity. The Sneads would buy meat downtown at Bressons, take it across the street to Grosjeans, order other foodstuffs, and have them deliver it all up the hill. "The Grosjean delivery truck got a workout, and would really be steaming when it got to the camp," said Tom. (Courtesy of the Dr. Thomas Snead collection.)

An early development of the Manor townsite, with curbs and sidewalks in place, looks down Bothin Road from the Olema Highway. Part of the Manor Station is visible at the center. Over a creek, the new bridge leads to the real estate office on Marin Road. (Courtesy of the Fairfax Historical Society collection.)

On a misty day in 1913, Olema Highway runs right to left at Manor Road. The sign, at the future entrance to the subdivision on Manor Road, reads "Manor Townsite—Oil Macadam Streets—Concrete curbs and Sidewalks—sewer— gas— water— Best Improved Subdivision in Marin County." (Courtesy of the Fairfax Historical Society collection.)

The Victoria Memorial Home was located on a 10-acre plot, just west of today's White Hill School. It was purchased and opened in 1920 as a home for dependent British veterans of World War I. This photograph was taken on a special occasion, possibly the dedication, as the home could only accommodate 10 or 12 permanent guests. Note the trestle at right, bringing the trains close to the back door. (Courtesy of the Brian Sagar collection.)

This 1920s view from the hill above Marinda Oaks shows St. Rita's Church at lower left, the new Fairfax School above and across the highway, and Buon Gusto Villa at right. (Courtesy of the Fairfax Historical Society collection.)

A 1920s postcard shows the good life in Fairfax, this time a residential part of Fairfax Manor. Substantial summer homes will become permanent dwellings. (Courtesy of the Newall Snyder collection.)

The Barberis family bought two lots on the corner of Scenic and Manor Roads in 1912 and built this home in 1917, when daughter Marianne was four years old. The girl with the white bow in her hair is Marianne and she still lives in the home. She is standing next to her father, Marcellino, who was chief pastry chef for many years at the St. Francis Hotel in San Francisco, starting work there when the hotel opened in 1904. (Courtesy of the Fairfax Historical Society collection.)

Tina Pastori reigned as queen over 2,000 subjects at the July 4, 1912, festivities in Fairfax Park, which were acclaimed a "brilliant success." Her court consisted of king Roy Perry and maids of honor Lina Balangero and Anna Vonderheide. Their royal costumes—scarlet robes trimmed with ermine, which were said to be valued at over $1,000—were no doubt rentals. (Courtesy of the Fairfax Historical Society collection.)

Julia Arbini is Miss Liberty in another of the traditional celebrations on the Fourth of July, this time in 1916. (Courtesy of the Fairfax Historical Society collection.)

The lead float of the 1916 Fourth of July parade held Julia Arbini as Miss Liberty and Bert Grasso as Uncle Sam, doffing his hat to the admiring crowds. They are passing the corner of Bolinas Road and Broadway where the former saloon-turned-ice cream parlor announces "Ice Cream Soda—10 cents." (Courtesy of the Fairfax Historical Society collection.)

Riding on the back of a flatbed truck during the 1922 Fourth of July parade is the queen of the festivities, Eleanor Gianini, with Russell Grasso as Uncle Sam. (Courtesy of the Fairfax Historical Society collection.)

Built in 1921 by Frank Stoltz, Stoltz's Emporium, a neighborhood grocery store at 19 Sequoia, was one of few commercial enterprises out of the downtown area. Marita Stoltz is standing behind her children, Nellie, Mildred and Victor, in front of the original store around 1923. Located near the railroad incline, the Stoltz Emporium offered a convenient place for hillside residents to shop before going up the hill. (Courtesy of the Fairfax Historical Society collection.)

A year or so later, around 1924, the store underwent a face-lift and added a gasoline pump out front. Frank Stoltz, with his children Victor, Nellie, and Mildred, pose for this scene. The incline car is at the station to the left. Apartments occupy this site today. (Courtesy of the Fairfax Historical Society collection.)

On April 30, 1919, soldier William Treanor returned home from the war in France. He is greeted at the train station by his mother, Mabel Treanor, right, and a family friend. Maple Hall and Fairfax Garage are in the background. (Courtesy of the Fairfax Historical Society collection.)

In the 1930s, fishing was good right in the backyard if one lived on Dominga Avenue, as documented by Elmo Cozza's catch. At that time, Fairfax Creek ran behind and under the stores along lower Bolinas Road and Broadway and behind some of the houses on Dominga Avenue. And that's a true fish story. (Courtesy of the Henriette Cozza collection.)

Dedicated in 1919, Alpine Dam was the second dam built on Lagunitas Creek, creating a major source of water for a growing county population. Many of the workers, who came to Fairfax to build the Alpine Dam, stayed and became permanent residents. Many workers were of Italian descent, so the town was given the title "Little Italy." A third dam, Bon Tempe, was built in the 1950s between the Alpine and Lagunitas Dams. The above photograph is of Alpine Dam after it had been raised eight feet in 1924. The original sidewalk can be seen at the lower elevation to the right of the road, on the downstream side of the dam. In 1941, the dam was raised 30 feet to its present height, resulting in major changes to the spillway and more than doubling the lake's capacity. (Courtesy of the Newall Snyder collection.)

Imagine the sounds when 100 accordionists from around the Bay Area assembled in the park for a Grand Tombola in August 1937. It drew a standing-room-only crowd to the grandstand and track area. The audience was eager to hear the official musical instrument of San Francisco. (Courtesy of the Henriette Cozza collection.)

Music seems inherent in Fairfax, perhaps started by this man, Ricco Roffi, with his reputation as "the singing garbage man." Morning pickups would be accompanied by melodious (to some) operatic arias, in Italian of course, as he made his rounds through town. He started his business in 1928 with this sturdy 1928, airless tire Kleiber truck built in San Francisco. His business was still "picking up" in the early 1950s. (Courtesy of the Fairfax Historical Society collection.)

Melodious tunes were later belted out by this hometown barbershop quartet, seen here in the Fairfax Fooleries, a live theatrical production that took place on April 25, 1952, on the stage of the Fairfax School. Pictured, from left to right, are brothers Curt, Herb, Rad, and Bob Ingram, a most popular quartet. Music continues to be a part of life today in downtown Fairfax. (Courtesy of the Ingram family collection.)

Seven

SCHOOL AND CHURCHES

By 1876, there were 16 children of school age who lived within the Canada de Herrera property, but were attending school in the Ross Landing School District (in the vicinity of the College of Marin.) They were the children of 12 families who felt it was time to have a school closer to their homes. On February 10, 1876, the heads of these families filed a petition to county authorities to establish a new school district, and within a week their request was allowed. The new Fairfax School District would be within the boundaries of the Canada de Herrera land grant, with P. K. Austin, Salvador Pacheco, and George Hubbard elected as trustees two weeks later.

A school was quickly built on Butterfield Road in Sleepy Hollow, which served their needs until 1898 when increased enrollment created the need for a larger facility. A second school was built one-half mile south of the first, on Butterfield, between Willow and Meadowcroft Drive. Some of the increase in enrollment was due to the establishment of the orphanage at Sunny Hills in San Anselmo. This second school building lasted only five years, however. In January 1903, it burned to the ground.

The third school, a two-story structure with a large assembly hall on the second floor, was immediately built on the same site. The population in the Fairfax area was increasing and there was a need for a school closer to the children it would serve. In 1908, such a school was built on the San Rafael-Olema Highway, now Sir Francis Drake Boulevard, near today's St. Rita's Church—the fourth Fairfax school. More than 80 years after closing, a few local citizens remember attending this school.

It served its purpose until 1921 when an even larger and more impressive school, Central School, was built across the road on Broadway. It became a landmark until it too was replaced, vacated, and demolished in 1954. Two new schools built in the 1950s, Manor and Deer Park, absorbed the growing student population. Today Deer Park is closed and Manor and White Hill Middle School serve the needs of Fairfax elementary students.

In the late 1800s and early 1900s, the ownership of a three-acre plot of land, formerly owned by the Sais family, was being transferred to various parties through the valley. It finally came under the ownership of the Catholic church, and, in 1916, the first church in the Upper Ross Valley was built in Fairfax. It was established as a mission parish of St. Anselm's in San Anselmo and later became an independent parish. In 1947, the original church underwent a major renovation. It served the community well for 37 years as a place of worship In 1953, it was replaced by the present St. Rita's Church. As a parish hall, the original church now serves as an auxiliary space for banquets, meetings, festivals, and other church and community functions.

In 1913, plans for a Protestant church were begun and a Sunday school was established with classes held in the Fairfax schoolhouse. By 1920, funds were being raised to build a place of worship and, in January 1923, ground was broken for a new Protestant church. On April 29, the Community Church on Park Road at Frustuck Avenue was dedicated. In addition to serving as a church, it also provided a meeting place for many civic organizations such as the Native Daughters of the Golden West, the Boy Scouts and other youth groups, and the Masonic Lodge. It was also the site of the first lending library and the first public school kindergarten. It served the entire community well until a new church was built in 1956 near Oak Manor, after which the facility was leased to other organizations. The building was razed in the 1990s to make way for the present housing project on the site and adjacent properties.

This is the first Fairfax School, built in 1876 on Butterfield Road in today's Sleepy Hollow. The entire student body—26 students and 3 adults—are all unidentified. This school would house students for only two years, after which increased enrollment demanded more room. (Courtesy of the Fairfax Historical Society collection.)

Tree-lined Butterfield Road runs from right to left to the intersection with the San Rafael-Olema Highway at upper left. When the second school, built in 1878, burned to the ground in 1903, this third school, center, was immediately built on the same site. (Courtesy of the Fairfax Historical Society collection.)

The third school was an impressive and substantial structure, with classrooms on the first floor and a large meeting hall above. This school served San Anselmo students after a fourth Fairfax school was built in 1908. Eventually it was replaced by other schools in San Anselmo and vacated in 1914. In 1916, it burned down. (Courtesy of the Newall Snyder collection.)

Around 1905, 42 students and one teacher pose for the traditional school photograph in front of the third Fairfax school. This is only part of the 110 students enrolled in 1905, possibly only the upper grades. The only identified person in the group is Clementina (Tina) Pastori, far right back row, a small child at the age of 11. In June 1909, she was the only graduating student at the fourth Fairfax School. (Courtesy of the Fairfax Historical Society collection.)

The fourth Fairfax School was built in 1908 just east of the site for St. Rita's Church on the highway, now Sir Francis Drake Boulevard. Total enrollment in June 1909 was 27 students. (Courtesy of the Fairfax Historical Society collection.)

In 1909, parents of students, teachers, and civic-minded townspeople gathered at the school and spent the day beautifying the grounds with rakes, shovels, and brooms and enhancing a feature of the town in which they had great civic pride. Perhaps some of the students were coaxed into helping. (Courtesy of the Fairfax Historical Society collection.)

The entire student body, pictured from left to right in 1911, is (first row) Marty Blagg, Ferdinando Ongaro, Andrew Peri, John Ongaro, Mario Arbini, Herbert Nelson, Charles Peri, and Josephine Arbini; (second row) Josephine Bresson, Irene Balangero, Mildred Treanor, Eva Regalia, and Marguerite Linsley; (third row) Otis Miller, Buck Peters, George Bernard, Clara Frustuck, Lilly Arbini, Annie Regalia, Lillian Knowland, Agnes Linsley, Meta Bolte, and Edna Nordholz; (fourth row) Emilie Balangero, Mary McAdams, Isabel Jory, George Niven, Georgiana Silveira, unidentified, Anna Vonderheide, Anita Peri, Manuel Silveira, Raymond Miller, Joe Silveira, Louis Regalia, and John Blagg. (Courtesy of the Fairfax Historical Society collection.)

In 1921, a new and larger school was built across Sir Francis Drake Boulevard on Main Street (Broadway), seen here around 1938. Note the bleachers to the left facing the running track, built in the mid-1930s to accommodate 1936 Olympic athletes who practiced here before the competitions. (Courtesy of the Fairfax Historical Society collection.)

The 1934 first grade class, from left to right, line up for their first class photograph as follows: (first row) Roberta Long, Lola Giorgi, Elsie Foglia, Bobbie Miller, Marjorie Buchwald, Roey Rossi, and Diane Schiller; (second row) unidentified, John Norton, Frank Klineman, unidentified, Victor Pizzaro, Eileen Baughman, Tally Stevenson, and Yolanda Boraccio; (third row) Bob Camiccia, Val Giorgi, Bill Maier, Ted Kohler, Claire Foley, Lois Bauer, and Barbara Foster. (Courtesy of the William Maier collection.)

By 1941, the Fairfax School had a band. Instrumentalists, from left to right, are (first row) Jim ? and Bob Neuman; (second row) unidentified, Kenny MacInnes, Dick Wells, four unidentified, Bill Maier, and Bob Starr; (third row) Miss Small (teacher), Roey Rossi, unidentified, unidentified, John Hurt, and two unidentified. (Courtesy of the Fairfax Historical Society collection.)

The fifth Fairfax School is seen here toward the end of its 33-year existence, with ivy about to engulf the building. It was considered seismically unsafe, so a new building was added at the rear of the property, and the older building was torn down in 1954. Much of the stone wall still exists along the sidewalk on Broadway. (Courtesy of the Fairfax Historical Society collection.)

The first church in Fairfax, St. Rita's Church, served not only the local residents, but also an influx of summer visitors during its early years in a growing Catholic community. In 1916–1917, 54 new homes were built in Fairfax and the town had more summer visitors than any other part of Marin, most likely due to the continued popularity of Fairfax Park. (Courtesy of the Newall Snyder collection.)

The interior of the original church is pictured in 1947 before extensive remodeling. The open-framed wooden trusses of the cathedral ceiling lent a sense of spaciousness to the humble church. (Courtesy of the Fairfax Historical Society collection.)

This photograph was taken in 1938 by Dr. Thomas Snead during the wedding of Mr. and Mrs. William Francis Allen. (Courtesy of the Dr. Thomas Snead collection.)

Very straightforward in design, the Community Church on Park Road served many purposes for the citizens of Fairfax, from 1923 until 1956. (Courtesy of the Newall Snyder collection.)

Among the civic groups that held meetings in the Community Church were the Boy Scouts, first organized here in 1917. Members of Troop No. 7, pictured from left to right in 1947, are (first row) Roger Muldavin, unidentified, Jack Forester, Bob Cortelyou, Don Kilgore, unidentified, and Norman Harris; (second row) Jess Bardness, Richard Fernly, Jack Terwilliger, Jim Bard, Ray Forester, Bob Haz, Gordon Chan, and unidentified; (third row) Sonny Sturges, Charles Massen, Wesley Kilgore, Don Erdman, Mr. Cortelyou, unidentified, Bert Carpenter, ? Morill, unidentified, Lou Ratzo, and Jim Wilkersham. (Courtesy of the Fairfax Historical Society collection.)

In 1948, on its 25-year anniversary, this unique view shows the Community Church in winter, with a light dusting of snow on the ground and trees. (Courtesy of the Fairfax Historical Society collection.)

Eight

THE INCLINE RAILROAD

When Messrs. Holt and Gray of the Fairfax Development Company considered putting the Fairfax Manor Heights properties on the market in 1912, they anticipated some reluctance by buyers to purchase hillside lots, with the inherent difficulties of access. Edward Holt came up with a brilliant solution—build an incline railroad to reach the top of the subdivision for easier access to the homesites. He got the idea from a European trip, where he had seen several such installations operating successfully.

Holt and Gray formed a new corporation, the Fairfax Inclined Railroad Company, and proceeded with construction. Publicity in Bay Area newspapers gave the public the idea that something unusual in subdivisions was about to happen, arousing much interest in the project. Ten thousand shares of stock in this new corporation were offered for sale and Fairfax Development Company bought them with the intent of turning them over to the buyers when all the lots had been sold, thus making the railroad a public utility owned by residents of the subdivision.

This never happened, however, for the developers did not sell all the lots. In 1919, they sold the remaining lots as well as their interest in the railroad to the Rivers Brothers. They in turn sold the railroad to August Seidel, who defaulted on his payments. Rivers Brothers then sold it to H. M. Ballou, who sold to Julius Hochfelder. When the line closed in 1929, Hochfelder was the owner.

Construction of the incline started in late 1912 or early 1913 and was a major project on Manor Hill. It climbed 500 feet in elevation, with a run of 1,500 feet and an average slope of 33 percent. Beginning at Sequoia Road, there were stops at Spruce (then Oak), Tamalpais, Scenic, and Upper Scenic at the top.

There were two sets of steel rails on the ties. The outer rails carried the car with a capacity of 26 passengers and the steel counterweight rolled on the inner rails. The car and weight were connected to opposite ends of a continuous cable, controlled by the powerhouse at the top of the run. As the car ascended, the counterweight would descend and roll under the car at mid-point. The counterweight equaled the weight of the empty car so the work of the motor was to handle only the weight of passengers, which would vary with each trip. A motorman on the car operated the system via electric connections to the powerhouse.

The grand opening on August 16, 1913, attracted a large crowd with much fanfare, speeches by local dignitaries, and the St. Vincents Boys' School Band in attendance for a musical send-off for the first trip.

The developers' advertising stated, "Every lot is within a 10-minute level walk from an incline station." Not exactly true, but it sounded good enough that buyers came forth. When a person bought a lot, he was given materials to build a tent on the site and many did just that, camping out for a year or so while they built their summer homes, many of which became the permanent homes now on Manor Hill. Rides were 5¢ each way, but commuters could buy a 100-ride ticket book for $2, only 4¢ per round trip.

After 1920, a tavern was built at the top of the line, which in 1928 offered a chicken dinner for $1.50. On May 26 that same year, an outdoor dance floor was inaugurated with a fee of 75¢ per couple. The view was inspiring and well worth the trip. The owner, Mr. Hochfelder, even inaugurated taxi service from the depot to bring patrons to the hill.

The early tales of clandestine activities at the tavern claim that it was once a speakeasy and a brothel and maybe even a gambling establishment. This is entirely possible because of its remote location. When word would leak out that the law was about to make a raid, someone down on the flats would phone the tavern to alert them and, by the time the officials reached the tavern, a 10-minute climb up the narrow crooked roads, it had been transformed into a perfectly proper and legal business.

In time, the foundations of some of the support timbers for the tracks began to settle, causing the car to lean as it passed over a particularly high point on the line. This was unnerving, to say the least. The State Railroad Commission condemned the system in 1929 and closed it down. Property owners were unsuccessful in trying to raise funds to make the necessary repairs and salvageable materials were sold for scrap in July 1930. Rails and equipment were removed and a year later the ties and timbers were cut up and sold for firewood. Thus ends another chapter of Fairfax history.

A few concrete pier foundations along the right-of-way and a row of telephone poles are the only reminders of where the railroad once was, from near 11 Sequoia Road to Upper Scenic where the former tavern is now a private home. All are gone, but not forgotten.

In late 1912, work was started on a project that would bring some degree of fame and fortune to Fairfax. The construction of the Fairfax Inclined Railroad was publicized throughout the Bay Area as a most unique undertaking, and its comletion was eagerly anticipated. Some degree of fortune fell to the developers, as lots were sold and houses were built on Manor Hill. (Courtesy of the Fairfax Historical Society collection.

In the spring of 1913, construction of trestles for the ties and rails is nearly complete. The sign reads, "This is the starting point of the FUNICULAR-INCLINE RAILROAD. 1500 ft. 500 ft. RISE—Operated by electric power—FAIRFAX MANOR is first in everything." (Courtesy of the Fairfax Historical Society collection.)

There are great views of the hills, across the valley from the second stop, about halfway up the line. The large cluster of bushes at right center is where Fairfax Lumber will soon be built. The San Rafael-Olema Road is just beyond it. The roads beyond this main thoroughfare are in Fairfax Heights, early in its development. (Courtesy of the Fairfax Historical Society collection.)

The trestlework allows the incline to pass over Tamalpais Road near Berry Trail. It is difficult to believe that this is a two-way road, not much wider today. (Courtesy of the Fairfax Historical Society collection.)

Men are working on the equipment and machinery that will make the system operate from the top of the line. A building the size of a one-car garage will soon cover it. Electrical connections from motors to the car will allow the motorman to control its movement. (Courtesy of the Fairfax Historical Society collection.)

Around June 1913, the ties and rails are in place and the car has just been put on the tracks, ready to have the cables, which will pull it up the hill, attached. For the grand opening in August, only the platforms have to be built to complete the installation of the incline railroad. (Courtesy of the Fairfax Historical Society collection.)

An early trial run by company officials, to test its operation, ran from Sequoia Road to Upper Scenic. The empty lots will soon be covered with homes. Azalea Avenue is at the upper left. (Courtesy of the Fairfax Historical Society collection.)

On August 16, 1913, the grand opening was marked with the inaugural run of passengers on the railroad. The St. Vincent 40-piece band, as well as interested spectators, gave them a rousing send-off. Dedication ceremonies were held at the park at the top of the line. Some of the crowd arrived on foot from the train depot, just a few blocks away; some came by horse and buggy; and same came in an automobile. (Courtesy of the Fairfax Historical Society collection.)

Somewhere along the line, the car descends through the trees on a sunny afternoon. (Courtesy of the Fairfax Historical Society collection.)

This is opening day at the top of the incline, with the power/machinery house seen at left. A walkway leads to the car where passengers are waiting to board for the return trip down the hill. There is still some construction debris to be cleaned up. (Courtesy of the Fairfax Historical Society collection.)

Sometime after 1920, a happy crowd is pictured at the upper end of the line near the tavern. On May 26, 1928, an outdoor dance floor called Moon Beam opened. Some local residents remember paying a nickel to ride to the top to buy an ice cream treat. Others recall walking all the way to the top to save their money. (Courtesy of the Fairfax Historical Society collection.)

The Fairfax Realty Company built a sales office to offer information and sell lots to interested visitors. The house at upper right is on Spruce Road, the first stop for the car shown pausing at the platform in the 1920s. (Courtesy of the Newall Snyder collection.)

When passengers stepped off the train at the depot, they couldn't miss the incline on the hill, just a few blocks away to the west. The white car is near the streetlight, and the tavern is at the top. This photograph was taken sometime after 1920, when the tavern was built. The right-of-way has been completely hidden by tree growth over the past 75 years. (Courtesy of the Newall Snyder collection.)

Nine

MOVIE MAKING

Before Hollywood became the film capital of the country, Fairfax already had the cameras rolling. In 1909, realizing that Chicago was not the appropriate background for the Westerns he was beginning to produce, G. M. Anderson set out from Chicago to seek the ideal locale. His Essanay Film Manufacturing Company worked its way across the country—Colorado, Texas, and Southern California—eventually coming north to Los Gatos in late 1910 and early 1911, before arriving in San Rafael on May 31.

Anderson, known as Broncho Billy, set up headquarters in San Rafael near Second and Irwin Streets. Their studio and film laboratory was a railroad boxcar parked on a siding nearby. Gilbert Anderson was the "A" in S and A (Essanay). His partner in business was George Spoor, who managed their Chicago studio.

On July 22, 1911, their first Marin-made movie was released, followed by a steady stream of one-reelers and one and two features each week until the end of the year. They produced 46 movies in the seven months they were located in Marin County.

Anderson became the first Western movie hero when he produced the Broncho Billy series, with himself as the star. The movies became very popular across the country and abroad. While in Marin, he would often bring his crew and equipment to the Fairfax area for its old-time Western atmosphere. When there was the need for more horses and riders than he had in his company, he would hire local people to fill in.

One of Fairfax's early longtime citizens, Frank Healion, used to reminisce about "riding for Broncho Billy" while he was growing up. He was living on the Roy Ranch, site of today's White Hill School, and riding a horse was second nature. He was paid 50¢ per day for joining the film company and performing as directed, but said he would have done it for nothing as it was so much fun. He was 20 years old at the time.

Anderson was most generous in donating his and his company's time by staging benefit vaudeville shows, both in San Rafael and in Fairfax Park. They would also show films in Fairfax Park for the townspeople. Some of his films showed scenes of downtown Fairfax, such as a stagecoach coming down Bolinas Road and stopping at the saloon on the corner at Broadway.

When Essanay left Marin in January 1912, the company spent three months in Lakeside and, in April, established their permanent location across the bay at Niles where Charles Chaplin joined them for five movies, including *The Tramp*. Although there were articles in local newspapers stating hopes that the company would return to Marin, it never happened. Several original copies of Marin-made Essanay films exist in the Library of Congress and in European archives; they have been shown at film festivals in Niles in recent years.

In 1913, another director/producer came to Fairfax and established a studio right in town. It was James Keane who built his new studio, the United Keanograph Film Manufacturing Company, on a six-acre plot of land at the east end of Mono Avenue. He solicited and received financial backing from several local citizens, including Henry Frustuck, Fred Croker, and Prentis Gray as well as Fairfax capitalists and developers.

In 1914, Keane produced a seven-reel feature movie entitled *Money*. The movie premiered on September 2 at the Savoy Theater in San Francisco with high acclaim from viewers. On September 19 and 20, a showing was held in the studio in Fairfax as a fund-raiser. The following year, on February 28, it was shown once in San Rafael at the Lyric Theater. No trace of the movie remains today.

Contrary to its title, the movie lost money and investors did not fare well. Keane was said to have some artistic talent, but little business ability. Although local reviews of the film were complimentary, trade journals were not and gave it mixed reviews, mostly negative. James Keane moved on and the studio stood empty for several years. Dreams of Fairfax becoming a film capital seemed just that—dreams.

In time, Hollywood became the movie capital and drew investors who were serious about longtime commitment to the industry. Fairfax and Broncho Billy may still lay claim to building the foundation for greater Westerns to come.

In 1914, the Pageant Film Company of San Francisco made a promotional film for the 1915 Panama Pacific International Exposition. Parts of the movie were filmed throughout the Bay Area. Here a camera crew is set up in the Deer Park area of Fairfax, awaiting the arrival of a stagecoach. The scene was captured by Henry Frustuck, an early Fairfax entrepreneur and developer. (Courtesy of the Frustuck-Sanborn collection.)

This scene of a runaway stagecoach, from the 1911 Essanay movie, *Broncho Billy's Christmas Dinner*, looks up Bolinas Road from the corner of Bolinas and Park Roads. A runaway stagecoach with a lone passenger, a young lady, is racing down the road and will soon be rescued by Broncho Billy. All did not go as planned though, for the stagecoach overturned on a sharp curve near Deer Park and the actress, Edna Fisher, was thrown to the ground, suffering a sprained ankle and a few bruises. (Courtesy of the Fairfax Historical Society collection.)

The Fairfax Park Annex, a saloon on the corner of Bolinas Road and Broadway, was shown in several Essanay movies made in Fairfax in 1911. On the porch are Henry Frustuck, an unidentified man (possibly the bartender), Fred and Bill Bridges, and an Essanay actor, complete with six-shooter. (Courtesy of the Frustuck-Sanborn collection.)

When was the last time anyone saw a stagecoach coming down Bolinas Road bringing a schoolteacher to Fairfax? Perhaps in December 1911, when this scene was made for the movie *Broncho Billy and the Schoolmistress*. It shows the stage approaching the corner of Bolinas Road and Broadway. The saloon was "Pipples Hotel" in this movie, where the schoolmistress would be staying. (Courtesy of the Fairfax Historical Society collection.)

Another scene from the same movie shows Broncho Billy, right, in front of the "hotel," considering a scheme to trick the schoolmistress. The plan backfires and Billy's rival for the affection of the schoolmistress, left, is run out of town. (Courtesy of the Fairfax Historical Society collection.)

A Thrilling Melo-
drama Full of Action
and Incident

"MONEY"

A glimpse of the future,
produced by
UNITED KEANOGRAPH
FILM MFG. CO.,
Fairfax, Cal.
Scenario written and
pictured by
JAMES KEANE

Featuring
Carlotta de Felice

In 5 Acts
Released February 1

An ad for the movie *Money*, a full-length feature film made in Fairfax in 1914 by United Keanograph, depicts the film as a melodrama/social movie featuring "employer-employee relations, kidnapping, lechery, self-sacrifice, anarchists, chases, labor violence, rescues, and unrequited love." This sounds almost like a present-day soap opera, but not exactly typical of Fairfax. Or was it? (Courtesy of the Fairfax Historical Society collection.)

In 1914, Julia Arbini, left, is pictured with unidentified friends near the movie studio at the east end of Mono Avenue. The "No Smoking" sign was wise advice given the explosive nature of nitrate film used in movie making at that time. In 1915, Julia became the Fairfax postmaster. (Courtesy of the Fairfax Historical Society collection.)

On May 22, 1914, the annual banquet of the San Francisco Motion Pictures Exhibitor's league took place at Pastori's Restaurant. Pictured here, from left to right, are James Keane, director/producer of *Money*; Carlotta de Felice, actress and Keane's wife; Ephriam Asher, later a producer at Universal Studios; Sol Lesser, president of the Golden Gate Film Exchange in San Francisco; Hattie Grunauer, Sol's Mother; and Mrs. Sol Lesser. The event drew hundreds of movie industry persons and their families, with games for the children and dancing with a six-piece orchestra after a highly acclaimed dinner. (Courtesy of the Julian Lesser collection.)

Looking down on central Fairfax in the 1920s, the large barn-like structure (upper right) is the former Keanograph studio at the end of Mono Avenue. The large white building at lower left center is the back of the Alpine Building on the corner of Broadway and Bolinas Road, the structure that replaced the saloon seen in the Broncho Billy movies. (Courtesy of the Fairfax Historical Society collection.)

Ten

HILL FARM
AND AREQUIPA

Two institutions that had a profound effect on the lives of many around the Bay Area are considered part of Fairfax history—Hill Farm and the Arequipa Sanitorium— although they are on the outskirts of the town proper. These institutions were the culmination of the interest and efforts of three outstanding persons who dedicated much of their lives to helping others.

Elizabeth Ashe spent much of her life as a nurse in San Francisco, taking care of the underprivileged. She saw the need to find better surroundings for them where they could recuperate from squalid living conditions and illnesses. Working with the Telegraph Hill Association, Ashe spent much time traveling between San Francisco and Ross, where Mrs. John Kittle had donated the use of a cottage on her property for housing up to six children needing a better environment. Miss Ashe describes an important event: "In the Summer of 1903 much of my time was spent traveling back and forth on the Sausalito Ferry conducting children to the Ross home. On one of these trips, I was seen carrying a small boy in my arms by Mr. Henry Bothin, who sought an introduction to me. He sat beside me to the journey's end, asking me innumerable questions. He learned from me that my little patient was a victim of infantile paralysis. It was not very much later that he confided in me that his only son had died from that dread disease. Mr. Bothin's interest continued to develop, and before the summer was over, he promised to place at my disposal a tract of land in Marin County, two miles from Fairfax. I drove out with him in his buggy to see the place and was entranced by the possibilities. It was an ideal site for our needs."

Henry Bothin lived in a palatial home in Ross and was one of the richest men in California at the time, thus was well able to offer land and financial assistance to this cause, which he did.

The property, which became Hill Farm, is today's site for the Henry E. Bothin Youth Center. Gradual improvements were made to the property and Hill Farm became a summer home for hundreds of recuperating women and children, administered by Ashe and other members of the Telegraph Hill Association. They tilled the soil and raised much of their own produce. A chicken farm was established, which became a source of income through the sale of surplus eggs. Henry Bothin would visit with the children every Sunday morning.

In 1910, Bothin gave Ashe and her association the title to 122 acres, Hill Farm, and another adjacent 35 acres to be used as a site for Arequipa Sanitorium, a new project, which had recently come into the picture.

Dr. Philip King Brown, and other physicians in San Francisco, promoted the idea for a tuberculosis sanitorium. The disease had increased among working women in that city since the 1906 earthquake. Brown, a good friend of Elizabeth Ashe, made his wishes known to her and she, in turn, interested Henry Bothin in the need for such an institution. He generously contributed funds.

The name Arequipa, a city in the Andes and a Peruvian Indian name meaning "a place of peace," fit their ideals perfectly. On September 4, 1911, the sanitorium opened, providing a way for afflicted working women to combat the disease "by removing these women from their urban environment and placing them in a situation in which they could rest and breathe clean air," as Dr. King stated.

Pottery was soon introduced as a means of keeping their minds and bodies active with a light occupation. Leading potters were hired to guide them. The pottery became better known than the sanitorium and their wares were sold in major stores across the country. Profits from sales offset much of a patient's expenses. Today Arequipa pottery is highly prized by collectors, is seen in many museums, and is recognized as an outstanding example of the Arts and Crafts movement.

The need for both institutions eventually diminished and, in 1955, the San Francisco Girl Scout Council signed a 20-year lease for Hill Farm and changed its name to the "Henry E. Bothin Youth Center." Arequipa closed its doors in 1957 as new drugs fighting tuberculosis made such sanitoriums unnecessary. In 1959, the Girl Scouts signed another 20-year lease for the Arequipa property, completing the acquisition of the acreage Elizabeth Ashe had received in 1910. In 1988, the Bothin Foundation gave the San Francisco Bay Area Girl Scout Council ownership of the property.

The three principals involved in the development of Hill Farm and Arequipa were, from left to right, Henry Bothin, Elizabeth Ashe, and Dr. King Brown. (Courtesy of the Fairfax Historical Society collection.)

This logo was embossed into the back of each of the 8,000 six inch by six inch tiles made for Casa Dorrinda in Montecito, neighbor to Santa Barbara, to identify their origin. Of course, now that the tiles are laid, nobody will ever see the backs. A similar smaller logo was also used on bowls and vases. (Courtesy of the Fairfax Historical Society collection.)

Hill Farm became a tent village shortly after the 1906 earthquake and fire and housed many refugees from San Francisco. The camp, with a staff of volunteers that included two doctors, three nurses, and two teachers, was open for six months and accommodated more than 260 displaced persons. (Courtesy of the Fairfax Historical Society collection.)

The original Hill Farm building, c. 1910, was located on the site of today's Manor Lyman House. (Courtesy of the Fairfax Historical Society collection.)

Built by Henry Bothin in 1919 with reinforced concrete, Stone House, or the "Woman's Building," was faced with stones salvaged from the construction of the nearby railroad tunnel bored through White's Hill in 1904. The house had 25 rooms and was advertised as "a convalescent home . . . at minimum cost to tired business and professional women who need complete rest, supervised sun-baths and a diet of rich milk, fresh eggs and home-grown vegetables. Rates, $1.50 per day." (Courtesy of the Fairfax Historical Society collection.)

In 1922, the Manor Lyman House was built. The left wing of the house was named for a member of the Bothin family. It looks much the same today as it did over 80 years ago, when it served as administration offices and living quarters for the children. (Courtesy of the Fairfax Historical Society collection.)

The Arequipa Tuberculosis Sanitorium for Working Women was the official name, with the main building at center, an administrator's home behind and to the right, and the pottery buildings to the left. Patients' rooms were behind the porches and were screened for maximum fresh air. (Courtesy of the Fairfax Historical Society collection.)

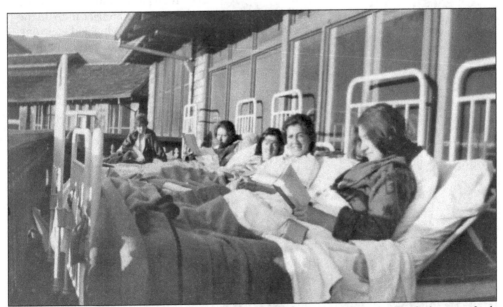

In warm weather, the porches were deep enough to accommodate the beds outside for more fresh air and sunshine. (Courtesy of the Fairfax Historical Society collection.)

They soon discovered that the land beneath them was a ready source of clay. Young men from a San Francisco orphanage were brought in to do the heavy work of digging and screening this raw material. (Courtesy of the Fairfax Historical Society collection.)

The young men did all the labor-intensive work to process the raw material and produce the clay. They also stacked and unstacked the kilns, before and after firing. (Courtesy of the Fairfax Historical Society collection.)

A view inside the studio depicts the great variety of shapes and sizes of pottery produced. Patients worked when they felt up to it, with no pressure to do so, and rested when they needed to. The patients all seemed to enjoy learning a new craft and some went on to become successful potters when they returned to a normal life. (Courtesy of the Fairfax Historical Society collection.)

The patients could sit out in the gardens and decorate vases and bowls while enjoying the good weather, something for which Fairfax was well known. (Courtesy of the Fairfax Historical Society collection.)

The Panama Pacific International Exposition of 1915 offered a good opportunity to publicize Arequipa pottery. A booth was set up where former patients demonstrated how pots were made on the wheel. (Courtesy of the Fairfax Historical Society collection.)

In 1917, the patients produced more than 8,000 tiles for floors in a large private home in Montecito, neighbor to Santa Barbara, with part of the brilliantly colored pattern shown above. It was much of the output of the pottery for the year. The design was by a local artist, Frank Ingerson, and the patients hand-painted approximately 1,650 individual tiles, which formed the borders around the perimeters of the rooms in which they were installed. The installation is still brilliant today. The home is now the administration building of a large retirement complex. (Courtesy of the Fairfax Historical Society collection.)

CPSIA information can be obtained
at www.ICGtesting.com
Printed in the USA
LVHW052252210222
711643LV00008B/163

9 781531 616984